THE MAKING
OF A PSYCHOTHERAPIST

Neville Symington

THE MAKING
OF A PSYCHOTHERAPIST

Neville Symington

Foreword by

Anton Obholzer

INTERNATIONAL UNIVERSITIES PRESS, INC.

Madison   Connecticut

Chapter 6, "Self-esteem in Analyst and Patient," reproduced by permission of The Australian Journal for Psychotherapy.

Chapter 13, "The Origins of Rage and Aggression," originally published in *Forensic Psychotherapy: Crime, Psychodynamics and the Offender Patient,* reproduced by permission of the publisher, Jessica Kingsley, London.

Extract from S. Freud, "On the History of the Psycho-Analytic Movement," *Standard Edition, 14,* pp. 1–66, reproduced by arrangement with Mark Paterson & Associates.

First published in 1996 by
H. Karnac (Books) Ltd.
58 Gloucester Road
London SW7 4QY

INTERNATIONAL UNIVERSITIES PRESS AND IUP (& design) ® are registered trademarks of International Universities Press, Inc.

Library of Congress Cataloging-in-Publication Data

Symington, Neville.
    The making of a psychotherapist / Neville Symington.
      p.   cm.
    Includes bibliographical references and index.
    ISBN 0-8236-3083-8
    1. Psychoanalysis.   2. Psychotherapist and patient.
    3. Psychoanalytic interpretation.   4. Psychotherapy—Philosophy.
    5. Psychotherapists—Psychology.   I. Title.
    RC509.S95   1996
    616.89′140232—dc20   96-43136
                                                CIP

Manufactured in the United States of America

FOR MIKE AND MANA

CONTENTS

PART TWO
Professional dilemmas

ACKNOWLEDGEMENTS

T his book is a construction made up of papers given to mental health professionals, especially psychotherapists, over an eight-year span in Australia and New Zealand, except for one paper that was given in India. My thanks are due to the organizations that invited me to give these papers, in Sydney, Melbourne, Adelaide, Newcastle, Auckland, Dunedin, and Bombay.

I should like to make special mention of Professor Russell Meares, who kindly invited me in successive years to give papers at the annual Westmead Conference despite the fact that my psychological outlook differed quite profoundly from that of many of the other contributors. This spoke well for his tolerance of differing points of view.

I should like to thank the Royal College of Psychiatry, which invited me to give papers in Sydney, Adelaide, and Newcastle. I should also like to thank Maurice Whelan, who invited me to be discussant to a paper by Brian Muir at a day's symposium on the Self held in Sydney; Professor Paul Mullen, who invited me to give a paper to his department in Dunedin; and Professor Graeme

Smith, who invited me to present a paper at a symposium on psychoanalysis at the annual conference of the Royal College of Australian and New Zealand Psychiatrists.

Thanks are also due to the Australian Medical Association, which invited me to contribute at a day's symposium on the Psychology of Crime, and, finally, to the Indian and Australian Psycho-Analytical Societies, which invited me to give a paper at their first joint conference in Bombay.

I have also been inspired by many groups of psychotherapists whom I have taught in seminars since being in Australia. The Queensland Psychotherapy Association, the Victoria Association for Psychotherapy, the Department of Psychiatry at Westmead, Ashburn Hall in Dunedin, and the New Zealand Association of Psychotherapy in Christchurch have all invited me to teach, and I have learned a great deal about psychotherapeutic functioning through all these teaching experiences. I should like to thank especially Dr John Adams, who invited me annually for many years to teach at Ashburn Hall in Dunedin, for both the opportunity and the warm welcome I was given there.

I would also like to thank Ms Liz Goodman, who moulded these papers skilfully into a book and without whose industry and patience the book would have never come into being.

I should also like to thank Mr Cesare Sacerdoti, whose enthusiasm encouraged me to produce this book. I would also like to thank him for his tolerance towards me and for undertaking various tasks that are normally the responsibility of the author.

Lastly, I should like to thank Joan, my wife, who read through most of my lectures before I gave them and always offered trenchant and useful criticism.

FOREWORD

Anton Obholzer

L   ike many a creative writer, Neville Symington has trodden
        a long and interesting path, something that is richly re-
        flected in this, his latest book. I have often thought that
a certain sense of social dislocation is a requirement for being
a social scientist—be it psychotherapist, psychoanalyst, psychologist, or whatever—the experience of dislocation giving a capacity
to stand outside the system and to observe it with a degree of
immunity to group pulls. If there is any merit in this thought, then
Symington's career, which has taken him from his birthplace in
Portugal, via England, to Australia, and with membership of the
Port Wine Trade, the Catholic Church, the Tavistock Clinic, and
the British Institute of Psycho-Analysis as stopping points, goes
some way to confirming this perspective. It also throws some
light on his capacity to take up a member role of various psychoanalytic institutions and schools of psychoanalysis, while retain-
ing his individuality and a wider perspective than is usual in

Anton Obholzer is a Consultant Psychiatrist and Psychoanalyst and is
Chief Executive of the Tavistock and Portman Clinics, London.

the followership of most psychotherapeutic and psychoanalytic institutions.

The result of these experiences is well captured in this book, *The Making of a Psychotherapist*—it is a record of a personal journey of professional development, but in sharing his "log book in the mind" with us, Symington gives us the rare privilege of seeing the many issues, both in the institutions and in the ideas that they purvey, that need rethinking and addressing, a process that is sadly often slowed down if not completely stopped by group allegiance and resistance to change.

This is perhaps where his life approach comes full circle— somebody who grew up "on the edge" of the system now describes the perspective from the edge of the psychoanalytic/psychotherapeutic establishment. It is rare for this sort of perspective to be organized into a coherent, thought-through, and thoughtful prescription—and one cannot call it anything else—for how one might conduct oneself as therapist and in exercising one's membership, and possibly leadership, of an organization in this field.

The approach Symington adopts is not without its risks, for in taking the stance of an individual approach, as he does, he runs the risk of re-enacting a particular role in the story of the *emperor's new clothes*, and whether his readers will then see the light or swat him remains to be seen. I for one firmly believe that books such as this need to be written, to be widely read, and to be discussed by trainees and trainers alike.

October 1996

INTRODUCTION

The contents of this book are based on papers that, over the past eight years, I have presented at gatherings of psychotherapists and psychiatrists, primarily in Australia and New Zealand. Some of the chapters are based entirely on single papers, whereas others, because of a commonality of theme or because an amalgamation serves to reinforce the points I put forward, are based on two or more. Whereas, for the most part, repetition within a chapter has been removed during editing, there is inevitably an overlap of ideas between chapters as I seek to advance an argument or illustrate a point. The opening paragraph of each "combined" chapter indicates its genesis.

In the early part of the book, I deal with the personal qualities that I believe are necessary to make a good psychotherapist. Inevitably, the question arises whether it is possible to *make* a good psychotherapist—surely, psychotherapists are born and not made? Although there is no doubt that some people have a natural gift and others just lack some essential quality, I believe that, if the basic potential is present, then it is possible to turn out a good psychotherapist. The titles of chapters three to six indicate those elements that I believe are absolutely essential, but I also touch upon these throughout the book and upon other important aspects of the psychotherapist's mental landscape.

In the second part of the book, in chapters eight to sixteen, I discuss psychotherapy in relation to such areas as modes of cure, conscience, ethics, and religion, and I challenge those theoretical models that, though seductive, are, I believe, ineffective. I do so in the full knowledge that some of my thinking is controversial. This is not to say that readers will not take issue with me on some of the statements made in part one, though I consider that part to be relatively non-controversial.

I also describe the identifiable phenomena that are familiar to the practising psychotherapist. It is the phenomenology of the psychotherapeutic encounter that I want to elucidate. My credentials for attempting this task are twofold. First, I have been a patient. Life has been kind to me, and I have not suffered those "blows of outrageous fortune" that have been dealt out to some. I have been in the presence of certain people whose individual cup of woe has been so great and so terrible that it has made me want to curse the gods who could have devised that organic development on Earth which we call "homo sapiens". However, as a patient, I had enough of a taste of it to get some inkling, with the help of the imagination, of what it is like for the sufferer in the process. I probably need not remind readers with a medical background that the word "patient" comes from the Latin *patior*, to suffer—the patient is the suffering one. Second, in the role of psychotherapist, I have had certain emotional experiences that have been for me a central and crucial element in the phenomena of the psychotherapeutic process. I cannot, of course, say for sure whether these have general applicability, though I know from speaking with colleagues that they have also experienced some of these phenomena. These, then, are my credentials, and it is from them that I speak. I shall endeavour all along to try to differentiate the phenomena from the understanding of them. As soon as we try to understand, we start to theorize; but although certain theories have helped me to understand certain phenomena, they have totally failed to elucidate others. Any theoretical speculation will be based on an examination of the phenomena—theory shall always be the servant of the phenomena and not the other way round.

In the eight-year period during which I wrote the text for this book, my thinking developed a very great deal. This thinking had two major sources of instigation: a new realization concerning the nature of mental life, and a growing awareness of a misconception that seems to lie at the very base of the psychotherapist's conceptualization of the therapeutic task. This misconception can be summed up as the belief that healing comes from the acceptance and validation of a patient's reality by his psychotherapist.

While I was lecturing at the Tavistock in London before migrating to Australia, I would often say in lectures: "If your patient gets upset, it just might be that the psychotherapist has made a mistake, been obtuse or insensitive." What I had said in London—what I believed to be a necessary caution—had become in Australia an overarching philosophy that was paradigmatic for all psychotherapists. In Australia, after a while, I found myself having to say the exact opposite: "If the patient becomes upset, it might just be that his psychotherapist has said something that is true but at the same time painful."* I also discovered that many psychotherapists believed that the treatment was a "corrective emotional experience" and that the curative factor in psychotherapy was the psychotherapist's own empathic understanding *in itself*. This belief is by no means restricted to Australia—one encounters it in all those countries defined by the adjective "Western". I am convinced that the consequences are disastrous. The most obvious consequence is that the psychotherapist believes that he is a saviour or god, or that through his own empathic understanding the patient will be healed. This has an obvious correlative, which is that other people in the patient's close emotional environment—

---

*Throughout the book, when I am speaking in general terms about people, both men and women are included. It is too clumsy constantly to use the two pronouns "he" and "she", or the adjectival "his" and "hers". It is high time that the English language settled on a personal pronoun, neither "he" nor "she", that could stand for both sexes. Having said this, I will reluctantly resort to "he" and "his" to stand for both sexes until the English language has caught up with current social developments.

parents, brothers, sisters, spouse, children—are all "baddies". This is a form of psychotherapy that tends to endorse and support the patient's own paranoid view of the world, which is: "All my misfortune is due to what has been done to me." There is no doubt that a person with such an inner paranoid structure will feel considerably better when his own point of view is sympathized with by an empathic person. When a paranoid structure remains in place below the surface, that person will always be dependent upon the support of others for his own point of view. Such a person remains emotionally without inner strength.

My own belief is that healing of a lasting kind is the product of an inner creative emotional act. This act is essentially free and cannot therefore be imposed upon the patient. It is my clinical experience that such an act will restructure the patient's reality and also his own perception of it. Although the experience of being accepted and having one's reality validated may help a patient towards achieving this emotional act, the process of acceptance and validation is quite distinct from it. I feel quite safe in saying, therefore, that if a patient's primary emotional figures have not changed in a quite radical way in the course of therapy, then that therapy has not achieved its purpose. At the beginning of my career as a psychotherapist, I did not believe that there was any intrinsic difference between psychoanalysis and psychotherapy. I thought that psychoanalysis was a more intense and deeper form of psychotherapy, and I thus differentiated between the two. I now think that the two processes are quite distinct. Understanding one's own mind is the goal of psychoanalysis, whereas the goal of psychotherapy is emotional healing. Emotional healing is certainly one of the fruits of the self-understanding gained in psychoanalysis, but it is not the goal. Therefore, although psychodynamic psychotherapy may *look* similar to psychoanalysis and derives its methodology from psychoanalysis, it is, in fact, a completely different process, with its own distinct goal.

The International Psychoanalytical Association has played its part in confusing these two processes. The desire to achieve self-knowledge and to understand one's own mind has never been and never will be a widely sought commodity. If the International Psychoanalytical Association were truly representative of this inherent reality of psychoanalysis, it would be quite a small organization. In fact, especially in recent years, it has been a rapidly expanding enterprise, blatantly imbued with missionary intent. The result has been an organization in which psychoanalysts and psychotherapists have been agglomerated under one umbrella. Also, frequently due to financial exigency, many analysts have taken into treatment patients who want therapy, not analysis. There is an urgent need for some diagnostic criteria that could be used to distinguish between those patients who want psychotherapy and those who want psychoanalysis.

This book is about psychotherapy, not psychoanalysis. It is based on my belief that psychotherapy makes use of certain techniques and theories employed within psychoanalysis in order to heal, and on my belief that no healing of a permanent nature can come from anything less than an inner creative emotional act. I felt for many years—long before coming to psychoanalysis, in fact—that reparative change comes about in the human being through such an inner act. However, I had not assimilated this piece of knowledge in such a way that it became central with an explanatory power of its own. This change of perspective can easily be seen as the reader progresses through these chapters.

I believe, as I say in the chapter on psychotherapy and religion, that the psychotherapy movement is in a state of crisis in the Western world. I think that this crisis in psychotherapy is part and parcel of a more general malaise, which can be attributed to the collapse of values—its practice is often harmful to individuals and it contributes to a lowering of values, those core values that have underpinned all the great civilizations for the last few millennia.

Neville Symington
Sydney
October 1996

PART ONE

PERSONAL QUALITIES

The emphasis in this section is upon the psychotherapist's own scrutiny of himself and the way in which he can, through identifying himself with a powerful imago and acting according to its prescriptions, fail to strengthen the patient's ego. In those patients who are narcissistic, there is *always* a self-destructive element—an inner situation in which a part of the self attacks, undermines, or sabotages the healthy part of the ego. When this inner *saboteur*, as Fairbairn called it, is projected into the psychotherapist who acts according to its dictates, then the patient never comes to grips with this fifth columnist within. Only when the patient does get a grip on this do his creative capacities within have a chance. As Jung (1933) says, "The patient does not feel himself accepted unless the very worst in him is accepted too." Therefore I am trying to emphasize the need for the psychotherapist to detach himself from a rigid omnipotent imago and not to allow himself to be controlled by it. However, originally I neither understood sufficiently the way the inner saboteur functioned nor interpreted it. I therefore correctly pointed out when the analyst had inappropriately donned the cloak of the saboteur, but I failed to trace the way that this had been brought about psychically by the patient's ego.

This book, though, is about a psychotherapist in the making, so both the strengths and errors of the psychotherapist are laid bare for the reader to scrutinize. I hope that this might help psychotherapists who are trying to learn, as I am.

CHAPTER ONE

The traditions and practice of psychotherapy

P sychotherapy means healing of the soul. Until the eighteenth century, the power to heal the soul was the prerogative of the "holy man". When someone was in spiritual distress, he approached a saint within Christendom, a Sufi within Islam, or an Arahat within Buddhism. What these holy people did when someone approached them in spiritual distress was to give the sufferer new understanding, a new line of thought that could then lead to an inner decision. Such a decision might either be to act in such a way as to alter the direction of habitual tendencies or, through reaching a deeper understanding of one's own personal sorrow, to be able to accept it. The following extract from *The Path of the Buddha* (Morgan, 1986) will illustrate my point:

> Kisa Gotami lost her only child and became almost mad with grief, not allowing anyone to take away her dead child in the hope that it might revive again through some miracle. She wandered everywhere and at last came into the presence of the Buddha. Buddha understood the deep sorrow that so blinded the poor mother, so after giving her comfort he told her that he could revive the child if she could procure a hand-

ful of mustard seeds from the house of one where no death had ever taken place. Hope came to her and she set forth from house to house asking for a handful of mustard seeds. She did receive, everywhere, the seeds with profuse sympathy. But when it came to asking whether there had been any death in the family, everybody universally lamented the loss of a mother or a father or a son or daughter, and so on. She spent hours travelling in search of the precious seeds that promised the revival of her son, but alas, none could give them to her. A vision arose before her and she understood the implication of the Buddha's hint. She understood that death is inherent in life which is the source of all suffering, all delusion. [pp. 22–23]

That vignette from the life of the Buddha is not only a good example of the belief that the holy man is able to heal the soul of the spiritually afflicted, it is also significant for the fact that he does not cure the woman but leads her in a direction that enables her to have a deeper understanding (Bion called this seeing something from a different "vertex"). The Buddha does not cure her in the way that a doctor cures his patient of a physical ailment.

It might be worth pausing a moment to look at the way healing came about in the story just told. We are told that the woman is "mad with grief", a grief that is more than she can bear. What, then, are the elements that led to her healing? First, we are told that the Buddha understood the deep sorrow (Kohut would call this "empathic attunement"). I think it is necessary to realize that this empathy is not something that can be learned—you cannot teach someone to be empathic. Empathy can be deepened through a personal emotional experience, but you cannot "learn" empathy. The next element is the therapeutic judgement that the Buddha makes. He judges that Kisa Gotami is blinded to the wider suffering (in modern parlance, he judged that she was in a narcissistic state) and decides to bring her into contact with the suffering of others. This emotional contact with others brings her into a new "sharedness" with the world. She learns a truth about the human condition, not by being told but through her own experience. This is the final element that brings healing to her.

Traditions in modern
psychodynamic psychotherapy

In his book *Man's Search For Meaning*, Viktor Frankl (1964) outlines his theory of logotherapy, which he derived from his experiences in two concentration camps. He tells of a woman whom he had in a logodrama. She was in despair. Having reached the age of 65, she felt her life to have been totally wasted; she was also bitter because her one son had been mentally handicapped. Through speaking with Frankl, the woman was able to endow the relationship with her son with meaning and came thereby to view her life in a different light.

In this very ancient tradition of healing, the individual's own moral decision is considered to be an important determinant of the state of his mental life. Jung followed very directly within this tradition. He quotes an occasion when he was treating a young man whose therapy and maintenance was being financed by an aunt. It emerged as the therapy was proceeding that this aunt was poor and was making considerable sacrifices in her own personal life in order to finance the boy. When Jung heard that his patient was going on expensive holidays at the expense of his aunt, he told the patient his treatment could do no good while he was behaving in such a self-centred way towards her.

Within psychodynamic psychotherapy, there are two separate traditions, which I think might best be typified by Winnicott on the one side and Melanie Klein on the other.

The Winnicottian school of thought

Winnicott believed that the early relationship between infant and mother determines the general character or style of the child's and the future adult's mental health: the child is not a separate individual entity from its mother, rather the child is merged with the maternal environment. Therefore, the nature of this environment is imbibed, as it were, by the infant. The individual's pathology in later life can be attributed to this early state of affairs for which he is not responsible. The psychotherapist's role therefore is to be in empathic understanding with his patient and to create thereby a new environment out of which a healthy ego can develop.

Winnicott's view is closer to the notion that an individual's pathology is something like a disease. In fact, Winnicott defined psychosis as an "environmental deficiency disease". The physician approaches the patient in such a way as to modify the disease state. In this way, Winnicott was very much in line with Freud, who always viewed pathological structures like a physician examining the symptoms of a disease entity. The tradition of Melanie Klein *in this respect* is also shared by Fairbairn and Jung.

The Kleinian school of thought

For Melanie Klein the infant is a separate individual from birth, with its own rudimentary ego. The conjunction of the two basic instincts—the life and death instincts—within the organism and the clash of these two instincts and the attempts of the infantile ego to deal with them are the source of enormous anxiety. The infant discharges its fears of annihilation and death out into the nearest receptacle—that is, the mother's breast. This then becomes the object of fear and anxiety because it has been so filled with hateful impulses. According to Klein, the individual has a moral responsibility for the state of his own mental health, and it is the psychotherapist's role to demonstrate this to the patient.

Modern perspectives

The perceived link between mental and even physical health and the individual's own moral acts is a very ancient one. It does seem that something like this occurred within the psychoanalytic tradition. Freud came to his discovery of psychoanalysis via neurology when he set himself up in private practice in 1886. The first patients who came to Freud all manifested very distinct and identifiable somatic symptoms, and, for a long time, patients who approached him for treatment fell into this category.

It was only very much later, when Wilhelm Reich wrote his classic work *Character Analysis* in 1933, that the perspective changed. It was now seen that what has to be addressed is the pathology rooted in the person's own inner character. The character is the structure formed by habitual tendencies, the inner heart of which are psychic acts. It was these inner psychic acts that were particularly developed by Melanie Klein—she referred to them as "phantasies". These are inner psychic acts that proceed from an active agent.

The psychotherapist following the Kleinian school of thought concentrates on what the patient is actively doing that causes his distressed state; the psychotherapist who follows Winnicott is aware of the unfavourable environmental circumstances of which the patient is a victim and sees his role principally as entering into feeling understanding of the patient's distress. However, both these positions are caricatures of Klein and Winnicott: they themselves did not act simply in this way, although some of their followers have done so.

In the extreme, therefore, the Kleinian psychotherapist persecutes the patient by placing on him a great deal of responsibility for the unfavourable outcomes in his life; the Winnicottian psychotherapist is so occupied with his patient's developmental misfortunes that he does not pay respect to the patient's capacity to alter things. Of course, approaches that accord with the extreme positions that I have designated will result in therapeutic failure.

The medical and moral positions

You will realize from the way that I have characterized these two schools of thought that the Winnicottian school is within the medical model that has developed in the context of the scientific traditions of the Enlightenment. What I have characterized as the Kleinian school is a moral position that comes out of a very much older tradition of mental healing. The principal figures who are within this moral tradition are Jung, Fairbairn, and Klein. Probably the most radical proponent of this view is Thomas Szasz.

Despite their big differences in other respects, they have all rejected Freud's particular scientific tradition and adopted the very much more ancient moral one. Jung quite specifically rejects the position taken by Freud and adopts a model of healing based upon values and a particular philosophical view of man. So, for instance, Jung said that the large religious denominations existing in the world today were in fact psychotherapeutic systems. Fairbairn rejected Freud's homeostatic theory of motivation and replaced it with the view that drives are intrinsically object-seeking. In this way, Fairbairn integrated drive theory with object relations theory in a theoretical way. Melanie Klein also adopted a similar position, though she retained the homeostatic theory out of, I suspect, deference to Freud. Winnicott similarly was angry with Fairbairn's critique of Freud.

It is one of the strange accidents of social development in history that, at the time of the Enlightenment, mental health in the western world passed from the domain of the church into that of secularized medicine. Freud, throughout his life, tried to explain his discoveries within the explanatory scheme of the Physicalist Tradition (described by Ernest Jones on p. 45 of his 1972 biography of Freud). I think it is George Klein (no relation or connection with Melanie Klein) who, in his book *Psychoanalytic Theory* (1979), has shown most clearly that within Freud's writings two theories run concurrently, one beside the other. On the one side, there is Freud's metapsychology, which is fully within the traditions of nineteenth-century science; on the other side, there is what George Klein refers to as Freud's clinical theory, which is quite different. The clinical theory is in line with the older tradition, consciously developed by Jung, Fairbairn, and Klein, and the metapsychology is within the traditions of nineteenth-century science and faithful to the ideals of the Enlightenment. Bettelheim, in his little book, *Freud and Man's Soul* (1983), points out that the medicalized strain that was already in Freud was very greatly exaggerated by his English translators.

The problems with theoretical models

Now I would like to discuss some of the practical effects of exaggerating either of these two models—the medical and the moral. Let us take the medical model first.

The psychotherapist finds himself confronted with a patient, the explanation of whose present distress is to be found in early misfortunes. What resources does the psychotherapist have at his disposal in order to offer his patient relief from his distress? The psychotherapist has none of the curative resources a doctor has, yet he is to be the instrument of his patient's cure. He has therefore to find a medicine within himself. He decides, in these circumstances, that the prime agent of cure is, to use an old-fashioned word, compassion. So the psychotherapist listens to the patient with sympathetic understanding, noting especially those traumata that have lead to his present suffering. There is no doubt that a sympathetic listening and an attempt on the part of the psychotherapist to understand the way in which external events have broken the foundations of confidence in the patient are an essential prerequisite of any therapeutic encounter. But is it enough? I think not. If the psychotherapist has not perceived the way in which the patient has actively contributed to his situation, then the patient will feel hopeless. Ultimately, the therapeutic endeavour leaves him as anxious as he was before it started.

How about the psychotherapist who operates within what I have called the moral model? If the psychotherapist focuses all his attention on nagging the patient, then this patient too will feel hopeless. People like the psychotherapist will have been nagging him for most of his life, and, on entering the consulting-room, he encounters a situation exactly like all the other social encounters he has ever known.

Conclusion

In every psychotherapeutic encounter, there are therapeutic forces and anti-therapeutic forces at work. It is the anti-therapeutic forces that generate the kind of interaction that I have character-ized—or perhaps it might be fairer to say, caricatured—in the moral and medical models. I believe that these models both pro-ceed from the same error. In the case of the psychotherapist who is persecuting, there will be something in the process going on between him and the patient that renders him ineffective. It is the same thing with the sentimental psychotherapist: he will listen sympathetically, but when it comes to an inner crisis, there is no robust emotional field of force to meet it. The patient will say that the psychotherapist is kind, but he will go away with his deeper problems unresolved.

If the psychotherapist does not understand the moral element to mental distress, then the patient will superficially sigh with relief but, at a deeper level, go away disappointed. There is no doubt that the theoretical models with which the trainee psychotherapist is equipped during the course of his training are essential tools of the trade. But of equal importance to this knowledge of theory is knowledge of when and how to apply it—which tool to use for a particular job. As the ancient tradition of healing has evolved into the modern practice of psychotherapy, much has been lost on the way. The psychotherapist must be equipped to meet the emotional conditions with which the patient has had to cope, such as separation, loss of the loved object, grief, and trauma. The recognition and understanding of these is a precondition for the psychotherapist's joining himself with the way in which the patient has had to struggle with these elemental dramas. I believe that this recognition and understanding can and must be achieved through education. We need to examine critically current teaching methods and training courses so that in the future those qualified as psychotherapists can, like the holy men, heal the souls of those in spiritual distress. However, it is the patient's own inner emotional creative act that brings healing to his psyche.

CHAPTER TWO

The psychotherapist's education

I follow Fairbairn (1958) in saying that emotional contact is what people most deeply yearn for and what fundamentally gives meaning to a person's life. Men and women derive their deepest satisfactions—in their work, hobbies, domestic life, and guiding aspirations—when they tap into the reservoir of emotional contact. Such contact, however, is only effectively made through a signal emitted from the true self of another. I therefore contend that the only interpretations that are effective are those that proceed from the true self of the psychotherapist. I am conscious that such a bald statement may be more acceptable to the reader if it is expressed negatively, that is, that interpretations that proceed from the false self cannot touch the emotions of the patient.

The requirement in many psychotherapy trainings that the would-be psychotherapist undertake personal therapy for himself is to assist him in reaching a knowledge of his true self and also to assist him emotionally to do so. The development of a person's emotional capacities is clearly central to any psychotherapy training, and without it all intellectual striving to master concepts becomes a hollow endeavour.

11

The question I want to address is: what is the intellectual formation that we require of a psychotherapist? What would be the intellectual programme best adapted to the particular functions that the psychotherapist is called upon to fulfil? Nearly all psychotherapy trainings are run on a part-time basis. Most of them are tacked onto the end of a long day, and, as Bion (1974) says dryly in one of his Brazilian Lectures, his own experience of this reminded him of nothing so much as a penitential exercise (p. 208). Many of us may have the idea, therefore, that to become a psychotherapist is an easy acquisition that can be tacked onto a psychiatrist's or clinical psychologist's training. Such training would consist of a nine-month module in the midst of many other training components, or it would be conducted continuously over a longer period though only occupying a relatively minor slice of time in the mental health professional's week.

All this tends to lead people to consider that becoming a psychotherapist is a minor professional role which anyone with a bit of good will and desire to help people can acquire without too much difficulty. I believe the very opposite is the case: that if it takes six years to become a doctor, then it will take at least eight to become a psychotherapist—and this would be eight years of full-time training and education.

The Academic Model of education

Imagine, then, that a new Chair of Psychotherapy has been created at the university and a professor has arrived to fill it. He has the task of devising the curriculum for the new intake of students who are due to start their eight-year training course in a year's time. Where will he start? He will want them to read Freud thoroughly so that they have a sound knowledge of all his writings. They will learn that Freud, starting as a neurologist, had a physical locationist theory of the mind and then moved on to a psychological theory. The students would learn the way Freud developed the Topographical Model of the mind and then the Structural Model, the way he changed his instinct theory and also his theory of anxiety. A sound understanding of his dream theory and of his conceptualization of the Unconscious, repression, transference, and infantile sexuality would also be acquired. Then the curriculum would include the way Freud's concepts were developed and expanded by the members of his early circle—Ferenczi, Jung, Jones, Adler, Stekel, Hanns Sachs, and Abraham—then to the way in which psychoanalysis spread to England, Germany, France and to the United States. The students would learn how, in the United States, Brill and Putnam had early influence, followed by the theoretical approach of Anna Freud and then the systematization of ego psychology by Heinz Hartmann. They would learn of the other developments in the United States through Erik Erikson, Mahler, Sullivan, and Horney; then they would move on to more recent times, with Greenson, Searles, Kohut, George Klein, Kernberg, and Roy Schafer. Back in Europe, the curriculum would include Melanie Klein, Michael Balint, Winnicott, Bion, Lacan, André Green, Rosenfeld, and many others.

The course would clearly include detailed study of infant development starting *in utero* and then birth (perhaps to include the birth trauma theory of Otto Rank and Freud's response to it) and all the developmental stages through latency, adolescence, and the different periods of adulthood through to old age and death. If it is true that in psychosis there is a recapitulation of pre-human stages of instinctual development, then the course would need to include zoology taken from an evolutionary perspective. The students will want a good grasp of physiological psychology with its psychological correlates, and then a good psychological grasp of the different functions of the mind: cognition, perception, motivation, and decision-making. The course would also need to include social psychology and sociology and, perhaps especially, those theorists like Jung, Talcott Parsons, and Bion who formulated the conjunction between individual and group psychology and were therefore link-persons between psychology and sociology. Those philosophers whose theories of the mind have so influenced our thinking about man would need to be included. There is no doubt, however, that much more would be necessary. We would expect such a course to include symbolization processes in the mind, affective life and the significance of myths, and a reasonably extensive knowledge of the important myths and their structure that have influenced races and the direction of their value systems.

Anthropology therefore would have a big place on this curriculum. As accurate use of language to describe complex emotional phenomena is the daily bread of the psychotherapist, the course would need to include a good selection of the greatest literature and poetry and also philology. As religion is such a powerful motivating factor in many human societies, there would need to be a religious studies section to the curriculum. What would give the course coherence would be its focus on the individual and group mind. Finally, the course would be clinically linked to a diversity of experience in the treatment of patients of different categories. I am sure that many readers can think of other subjects that would need to be included in this curriculum.

Here, then, is the outline for the education of psychotherapists. I would like to call this model of education the "Academic Model". Perhaps one day societies may begin to catch up with the present psychological needs of mankind. When that happens, then perhaps psychotherapy schools somewhat along the lines I have been outlining will spring up alongside the more traditional medical schools. But, even were these schools flourishing, would they provide what is needed for the would-be psychotherapist?

The need to discover the true self

Many of the most creative minds have had to break free of the stranglehold of the official academies of which they were members. I went recently to the Sidney Nolan exhibition that was on at the New South Wales Art Gallery, where I read that Nolan could find no resonance for his own soul in the official curriculum of the art school of which he was a member. So, instead of attending it, he spent hours in a library poring over books on Picasso, Matisse, Chagall, Cézanne, and others. Here he evidently found nourishment for his emotional self. I also found, in *Raoul Dufy* by Raymond Cogniat (1978), the following account of the moment when Dufy severed relations with the traditional approach of his own studio:

He went to the studio of Bonnat, but did not like the sombre atmosphere of that house. He did not agree with his conventional point of view, but was glad to have found a working place and some models without having to pay for them. One day he tried to express all the joy and the light of a beautiful red-haired girl, but was only criticized by his teacher, while the sombre work of one of his companions was highly praised. Raoul Dufy was then sure that there was nothing else he could learn at that school. [pp. 14–15]

When I was in my teens, I knew slightly an old man who told me one day that when he had been at school there had been a boy in his class who spent his time making paper aeroplanes of the most varied and intricate kind. He was the despair of his teachers. Then the old man smiled at me and said "That boy's name was De Havilland."

Nolan, Dufy, and De Havilland all had the courage to follow the inner light and break away from the official teaching academies of which they were a part. None of them would have achieved good marks since they were being true to themselves. If what I have said at the beginning is true—that the discovery of the true self is an essential prerequisite for a psychotherapist—then the student who gets a First at the end of his eight-year course at a school of psychotherapy is not necessarily a good psychotherapist. If his learning is academic knowledge alone, it will be valueless and have no functional significance in his work as a psychotherapist. The Academic Model, then, fails if a particular standard is set as an ideal for all.

Such a course as the imaginary one I outlined does not exist, but truncated versions of it do. I have come across many psychotherapy trainings that offer a standard selection of authors and particular subject-matter as the panacea for those wanting to become psychotherapists. They operate on the "Academic Model" without the virtue of its learnedness. They tend therefore to be narrow and elitist. This is partly because the attempt is made to pretend that it is possible to squeeze a psychotherapy training into a totally unrealistic time-frame. While the imaginary programme that I outlined above would fail essentially to meet the requirements of a psychotherapy training, the truncated versions of it that one encounters throughout the world are even worse. At least in the imaginary programme there is quite a big menu to choose from. Within it, a student might be lucky enough to find something that is congenial to his mind, whereas psychotherapy trainings as they exist today tend to offer a *table d'hôte* menu with only one dish that has to be eaten if the student does not want to go hungry. I think we need to think again, depart radically from the Academic Model, and take our cue from Nolan and De Havilland. I want now to outline what I will call the "Invention Model".

The Invention Model of education

It is a common experience that, as a person uncovers a new aspect of himself in an analysis, he will begin to want to study a new book or attend a course of lectures that had not previously held his interest. The instigator of this new flowering of intellectual interest is an inner emotional yearning—the analysis has caused a new emotional reality to exist within the psychological structure. The person in question then wonders what to do with this new emotional reality, which feels like a foreign body. So the desire arises to integrate it and bring it into relation with the rest of the psychic structure. I believe that to come upon this new inner reality is frightening, because it carries with it responsibility. Its possessor must declare ownership of it, and this is resisted. Why? Because it means a separation from those with whom the possessor hitherto shared a corporate sense of togetherness. He is alone, totally on his own. This is such a frightening experience that he is tempted to cover it over and rush back and seek the cover of warm togetherness.

To live by the guidance of an inner light is terrifying and is probably only possible for any human being for a few brief moments in the course of a lifetime. It means forsaking the support of those warm supportive figures in their outer environment and even more so of those in their inner environment. Frequently a patient will cling tenaciously to the most tyrannical inner figure rather than face isolated inner loneliness. I believe, in fact, that it cannot be done unless someone has the experience of being held psychologically. This is why Michael Balint (1968) in particular stressed the need for a patient in analysis to regress to a state where the analyst holds and does not intervene with interpretations—only an experience of that state can enable the patient to start a new beginning. In the absence of this psychological hold, the patient takes flight into conventionality. He feels comfortable again, supported, and no longer lonely. But he has lost a precious treasure that could have been the seed of something true, something genuine, something creative. To hide under the cloak of another is a great temptation to human beings, but it spells psychic death.

To follow the inner light in the way that Nolan and De Havilland did is the path that the would-be psychotherapist needs to tread. This will be his aim, despite all its difficulties. The developing emotional realities within become the guide to his intellectual development. It seems as if there are two paths, then: either the emotional self capitulates and passively submits to the intellectual structure imposed by another, or it determines to fit an intellectual structure to its own emotional shape. What I am recommending for the psychotherapist is the latter course, and it is this that I call the Invention Model. Passive submission to an already-made system of thinking is the Academic Model. Which model is operating is determined by inner realities. The following case illustrates how the Invention Model guided me.

An inner puzzle

A girl came to see me once, and in the initial interview she told me what a wonderful mother and father she had. She went into quite a rapture about her home. I took her into treatment, and it soon became evident that she had suffered severe deprivation in her home life. She had been sent away to boarding school at a very young age; her parents rarely visited her. When she came home for holidays, she was shown little love or care. Yet she clung to the illusion that she had had the most wonderful home life. I found it difficult to understand why she clung so tenaciously to this belief in the face of manifest evidence to the contrary.

I had at the time read a good deal of Freud and quite a bit of Jung and a few other psychoanalytic writers, but I had not come across an answer to this question. What is more, as time went on, I came across several other patients whose behaviour was similar. What was the reason for it, I asked myself? It was not the kind of insistent questioning that makes one go and look up references (and, anyway, under what subject would I look for it in the index?); it just lay there in my mind as an object of curiosity that puzzled me and for which I had not found a satisfactory answer. I knew, of course, that it was denial, but what purpose did the denial serve? That was the problem I could not resolve.

One summer holiday I took with me the novel *Middlemarch* by George Eliot (1872). I had not read George Eliot before and had been encouraged to read her by a friend whose enthusiasm for Eliot had touched me somewhere. I could not have told you *why* I was taking *Middlemarch* with me to read that summer, only that I knew for certain that I wanted to read it. George Eliot's delicate sensibility, range of understanding, and combination of vast knowledge with emotional sympathy with her characters is simply staggering. One of the sub-plots in the book is the disastrous marriage of Lydgate to Rosamund, a true *femme fatale*. Lydgate reaches a point where, although he recognizes that his wife does not love him, he holds on desperately to his love for her. "She will never love me much" is easier to bear, says Eliot, than the fear "I shall love her no more". And the context in which Eliot describes this makes it clear that Lydgate's self-esteem is rooted in his capacity to love rather than in the knowledge that he is loved himself. Fairbairn said that narcissism results from a turning away from the love object in abject disappointment. One might say, therefore, that Lydgate was fighting a desperate battle against being engulfed by a fateful narcissism.

Subsequent to reading that passage in *Middlemarch* and thinking about it further, I began to notice that a person's self-esteem is more rooted in his ability to love another than in the sense that he is loved: the latter is not such a desperate loss as the former. I further began to notice that often some sort of moral collapse ensues if the human endeavour to love is abandoned. I thought that perhaps here is the difference between the psychopath who commits murder and the obsessional's fantasies of murdering and his enormous anxieties that he might. In the first case, the endeavour to love as a motivating aim has been abandoned, whereas in the second it is still being desperately held on to. I had also noticed that there is a close association between a fearsome superego and the absence of an object that is loved. It also became clear why it was only when there had been a transference of love to the psychotherapist that the patient could evaluate his parents more realistically. When he was sure he had an object that he loved, it was safe to examine his family members critically. These understandings, which were sparked by George Eliot's deep understanding of Lydgate's distress of soul, brought with them another realization closely connected with it. I have come across patients who have had a shocking dose of misfortune in their upbringing, yet cling tenaciously to the image of maltreatment at the hands of their parents. It was the tenacious clinging that was the puzzle, even in the face of evidences to the contrary. It was the reverse of the other situation that I have just been describing. Then I began to see that such a person has to fight off the knowledge that he is loved because it reveals his own unloving inner state, and he cannot bear the guilt of it. This latter point, I have noticed, is frequently missed by psychotherapists who tend to sympathize with the patient in a sentimental way and thereby fail to come to grips with the awful truth of the inner situation.

The emotional signal

At the time, these truths seemed to me to be important both as an individual and also as a psychotherapist. The understanding came about as the result of an inner puzzle that was part of a spectrum of problems that I was at that time trying to solve. Illumination of these problems came about as a result of reading *Middlemarch*. I do not think it was random chance that led me to take George Eliot's novel with me on that holiday—something was attracting me to her at the time. I had sensed something that seemed important for me from the manner in which my friend talked of her passion for George Eliot. In my unconscious, then, an emotional signal was at work. I followed that signal, and it bore fruit in one area of knowledge. And it was the sort of knowledge that allowed my soul to grow.

It is possible to have knowledge that bears no relation to our emotional state of mind. In our enthusiasm for a new system of knowledge, we may believe that we are acting in accordance with it, but then certain discordant facts begin to reveal that our emotions and our intellectual knowledge inhabit two entirely separate universes. This is the prototypical false self situation, which comes about as a result of a passive reception of the Academic Model in whatever form it comes. We all require an inner searching activity so that our knowledge becomes assimilated to our emotional self in such a way that each reflects the other. It is only then that our knowledge becomes the possession of the true self and only then that knowledge finds its true function—the enlargement of the mind. The Academic Model is a system imposed from without which we inwardly submit to; it is of no value to the development of our minds. It may look impressive but it does not deceive the unconscious of the patient. On the other hand, the Invention Model has its source in the emotional quest of the individual. The guide is the inner emotional signal, and this model, I believe, is essential for the education of a psychotherapist.

Implementing the Invention Model

If we adopt this proposal, it clearly is a headache for those who are responsible for the education of psychotherapists. It probably means we need to overthrow the way we have been teaching psychotherapy. Would it be courage or folly to allow students to follow their own emotional signals and abandon any formal programme of teaching? On the other hand, is it right to restrict our programme to just a few authors, however great they may be? Is it not enormously limiting to offer to our students only the theories of official psychological thinkers when we know that all the greatest literature has been concerned with the inner motivating forces in the individual and in the crowd? Why did Iago plot Othello's downfall with such relentless intent? Shakespeare has a convincing answer that could be important to many of us psychotherapists. Why did old Karamazov clown so absurdly? Dostoevsky gives a convincing reason. Shakespeare, Dostoevsky, and George Eliot all had a "theory" of the mind, and it would be possible to distil it out from their writings. Our imaginary Professor of Psychotherapy is in a way right to offer all these alternatives, but, in the way it is presented, it cannot meet the emotional seekings of each individual. I also believe that we frequently try to make too sophisticated an offering to our students. It may not be folly but an act of courage to encourage students to follow their inner emotional signal. In that great classic on education, *The Idea of a University*, Cardinal Newman (1852) says:

> How much better, I say, it is for the active and thoughtful intellect, where such is to be found, to eschew the College and the University altogether, than to submit to a drudgery so ignoble, a mockery so contumelious! How much more profitable for the independent mind, after the mere rudiments of education, to range through a library at random, taking down books as they meet him, and pursuing the trains of thought which his mother wit suggests! [pp. 149–150]

I truly believe that such a procedure would introduce a better education for the psychotherapist than any Academic Model. It would mean much restructuring and some deep and penetrating thinking, but I believe that we require no less of our patients. It would, I am sure, improve the chances that the psychotherapist would speak from the True Self and thus make emotional contact with the patient.

Conclusion

In their unconscious, patients sense whether interpretations have been arrived at through internal struggle and resolution or whether it is just being passed on from master to pupil and pupil to patient. When a patient senses that an interpretation is the product of the Invention Model, he feels at a deep level the union of souls in a common endeavour. This mutuality is probably the single most healing factor in psychotherapy, as it enables the inner creative emotional act. If this is true, then the education of psycho-therapists needs to reflect this fact.

CHAPTER THREE

The analyst's inner task

I am sitting in my consulting-room and there is a knock on the door. I open it, and standing there in the doorway is a middle-aged lady with grey hair.

I shake her by the hand and I notice that she is wearing a red dress and black shoes. She pauses hesitantly and then rushes rather quickly to an armchair and sits in it. As I take my own seat, I detect the scent of Chanel No. 5. I had not met this woman before, but I have now touched her, seen her, heard her, and smelt her. These perceptual facts can be explained in terms of my sensory receptors and their link through the central nervous system to my brain. So I touch her, see her, hear her, and smell her, but I also *feel* her. I also know that she feels *me*. There is an interpersonal psychic experience whose physical correlate would be similar to two blind people feeling each other all over until each one begins to "know by feeling" the other.

The communication of feelings

When this woman came into my consulting-room, I received a very accurate feeling representation of her which became encoded in my inner affective representational life. But my problem is that I am not in touch with this inner representation. There is a barrier between my ego and this representation. This means that I have affective knowledge of this woman in my consulting-room, but I do not have conscious awareness of it. To illustrate from my own experience that such a psychic registration does indeed take place, I will relate an experience that occurred some years back.

A girl was referred to me after a suicide attempt. I took her history: her mother, her father, her siblings, her earliest memory, a recent dream, the important emotional experiences of her childhood, her adult sexual life, and the apparent reasons behind her recent suicide attempt. When the interview was nearly over, I sat back. I then had a feeling that prompted the following question: "Were there any other important figures for you outside the immediate family? Any grandparents, uncles, aunts?" She looked at me, her eyes narrowed and she appeared threatened. Then, after a moment, it changed to embarrassment and she said, "Of my four grandparents, three committed suicide."

Now, what was the feeling registration that had prompted my question? The feeling was blurred but quite definite: it was that I was in the presence of a young woman in a panic who was constraining my vision and pointing my head in a vice-like grip towards her mother, father, and sister, and, if I looked beyond, I would be turned into a pillar of salt, like Lot's wife. I have no doubt that I had received such a feeling from her. But when was that feeling registered in me? It was clearly there before I asked the question. My surmise is that the affective state was registered within the first minute of her being in the room with me. The role of the conversation that passed between us was to enable that feeling to emerge into my conscious awareness, to come to birth (the role of most social conversations is to prevent such a birth from occurring).

I want now to give an example of a patient who felt the inner act of her analyst. The woman I was seeing was in a psychotic transference.

It was close to Christmas and it had not been decided whether the sessions would end on the Tuesday or the Wednesday before Christmas. She had said something, and then my mind wandered; I found myself deciding which of the two days would be better. I said to myself that we would finish on the Tuesday. It was an inner thought and I was quite certain that it was contained within the confines of my own personal space. I was wrong. The moment I had decided she looked up and said, "You have just stolen something from me." There were two other occurrences when she found me out. Twice at the beginning of a session, after a pause, she said to me, "I can't start until you get that off your mind." On each occasion she was perfectly right. When within me there were obstacles to her analysis, she was able to feel them.

Inner psychic registration

I am presenting as a fact that there is a feeling communication that occurs between people who are present in the same physical space (I am leaving out of this discussion the possibility of telepathic communication when the two people are not in the same physical space). I posit further that this feeling registration extends to an individual's inner psychic activity—that even one's innermost thoughts are subject to registration in the mind of another.

You may think that I am talking of a rare phenomenon, but I believe that the very opposite is the case. I have just given two examples, but I do not think a day passes in which I do not observe an instance of it in my consulting-room. It is also clear to me that it is the fundamental mode of communication between human beings. It is at this level that human beings respond to one another. It is why one person is attracted to another, why I like A but not B, why I buy fruit in the shop next to the newsagent and not in the one next to the bank a bit further up the road.

Clinically, I have often had an experience like this one:

A young woman, Mary, who was a secretary, complained that her boss treated her contemptuously, that other secretaries dumped more work on her, that it was always she who worked overtime, that it was always she who was the last to get a pay rise, and so it went on. It was clear that she had a dreadful image of herself. She felt that she was just a useless piece of rubbish—and her social environment treated her accordingly. When I thought I might be late one day, I caught myself thinking: "Oh, Miss Z won't mind." I felt her as an exploitable object.

Then, through the analytical process, something shifted in this state of affairs. I began to feel her as someone worthy of re-spect. There had been a change of inner psychic registration not only in me but also in her own feelings about herself. She began to report that people treated her differently—her boss made a remark that denoted respect for her, she noticed that the other secretaries dumped less work on her, she found she was not working overtime so often and that, unlike in the past, she got a pay rise before the others.

Clearly, the people in her social environment encoded a differ-ent psychic representation of her. They acted differently to-wards her, though they were probably not conscious of it, and started to talk about her. One woman said, "You know what, I don't know what's come over Mr Jones [the boss]. He called Mary up to him yesterday and said she could have a half-day off next Friday and said she deserved it for all the extra work she'd been doing lately." Another said, "You know, this morn-ing I asked Mary if she would do a couple of my letters for me and, you know what, she said she was fed up of doing extra letters and that I could do them myself." I leave the other remarks to your imagination.

The unconscious possession

I believe it is possible to make sense of this phenomenon—that the people in my patient's social environment were quite unconscious of their changed psychic registration—if you accept that knowl-edge can be registered within the personality but not consciously possessed. When it is conscious knowledge, it is possessed in such a way that responsibility is taken for it, with all the succeeding consequences. Freud himself was in "unconscious possession" of knowledge at least once in his lifetime.

In his paper, "On the History of the Psycho-Analytic Movement" (Freud, 1914d), Freud relates how his conviction that sexuality was a significant factor in the aetiology of the neuroses met with a bad reception among his circle of friends in Vienna. However, as far as he was concerned, it was a field of investigation that merited more attention. He also found consolation

> . . . in the thought that I was taking up the fight for a new and original idea. But, one day, certain memories gathered in my mind which disturbed this pleasing notion, but which gave me in exchange a valuable insight into the processes of human creative activity and the nature of human knowledge. The idea for which I was being made responsible had by no means originated with me. It had been imparted to me by three people whose opinion had commanded my deepest respect—by Breuer himself, by Charcot, and by Chrobak, the gynaecologist at the University, perhaps the most eminent of all our Vienna physicians. These three men had all communicated to me a piece of knowledge which, strictly speaking, they themselves did not possess. . . . But these three identical opinions, which I had heard without understanding, had lain dormant in my mind for years, until one day they awoke in the form of an apparently original discovery.
>
> One day, when I was a young house-physician, I was walking across the town with Breuer, when a man came up who evidently wanted to speak to him urgently. I fell behind. As soon as Breuer was free, he told me in his friendly, instructive way that this man was the husband of a patient of his and had brought him some news of her. The wife, he added, was behaving in such a peculiar way in society that she had been brought to him for treatment as a nervous case. He concluded: "These things are always *secrets d'alcove!*" I asked him in astonishment what he meant, and he answered by explaining the word *alcove* (marriage bed) to me, for he failed to realize how extraordinary the *matter* of his statement seemed to me.
>
> Some years later, at one of Charcot's evening receptions, I happened to be standing near the great teacher at a moment

when he appeared to be telling Brouardel a very interesting story about something that had happened during his day's work. I hardly heard the beginning, but gradually my attention was seized by what he was talking of: a young married couple from a distant country in the East—the woman a severe sufferer, the man either impotent or exceedingly awkward. "Tachez donc," I heard Charcot repeating, "je vous assure, vous y arriverez." ["Go on trying. I promise you, you'll succeed."] Brouardel, who spoke less loudly, must have expressed his astonishment that symptoms like the wife's could have been produced by such circumstances. For Charcot suddenly broke out with great animation: "Mais, dans des cas pareils, c'est toujours la chose génitale, toujours . . . toujours . . . toujours." ["But in this sort of case, it's always a question of the genitals—always, always, always."] . . . I know that for a moment I was almost paralysed with amazement and said to myself: "Well, but if he knows that, why does he never say so?" But the impression was soon forgotten; brain anatomy and the experimental induction of hysterical paralyses absorbed all my interest.

A year later, I had begun my medical career in Vienna as a lecturer in nervous diseases and in everything relating to the aetiology of the neuroses I was still as ignorant and innocent as one could expect of a promising student trained at a university. One day I had a friendly message from Chrobak, asking me to take a woman patient of his to whom he could not give enough time, owing to his new appointment as a University teacher. I arrived at the patient's house before he did and found that she was suffering from attacks of meaningless anxiety, and could only be soothed by the most precise information about where her doctor was at every moment of the day. When Chrobak arrived he took me aside and told me that the patient's anxiety was due to the fact that although she had been married for 18 years, she was still *virgo intacta*. The husband was absolutely impotent. In such cases, he said, there was nothing for a medical man to do but to shield this domestic misfortune with his own reputation, and put up with it if people shrugged their shoulders and said of him: "He's no good if he can't cure her after so many years." The sole prescription for such a malady, he added, is familiar enough to us, but we cannot order it. It runs: "R. *Penis normalis dosim repetatur!*" I had never heard of such a prescription, and felt inclined to shake my head over my kind friend's cynicism.

I have not of course disclosed the illustrious parentage of this scandalous idea in order to saddle other people with the responsibility for it. I am well aware that it is one thing to give utterance to an idea once or twice in the form of a passing *aperçu*, and quite another to mean it seriously—to take it literally and pursue it in the face of every contradictory detail, and to win it a place among accepted truths. [pp. 13–15]

Barriers against
the analyst reaching his own feelings

In a certain stream of current psychoanalytic literature, we read such phrases as these: "I waited and then an interpretation emerged", "It may be a long time before a pattern begins to emerge", and "Then a feeling came up in me". These phrases all mean that we cannot become aware until feelings have some definable shape. It is only when they have a *form* that they can be apprehended and then named. Freud said that in the Unconscious there are no feelings. I think it would be more correct if he had said that in the Unconscious feelings have no definite form.

Transforming proto-feelings into feelings

The mind cannot conceptualize matter without form. Astronomers believe that after the Big Bang there was no atomic structure but only radiation—protons, electrons, and neutrons—and then slowly, under the powers of gravity, electromagnetism, and nuclear force, these elemental particles formed themselves into atoms. This is an analogy whose purpose is to orientate the imagination in a certain direction (because it is the imagination that governs conceptualization). Feelings in the primordial state are amorphous, having no form. It is a state of affairs extremely frightening to the individual. (Other analysts avoid this state of affairs by having an artificial form that we call a theory, which, by definition, will not fit any particular individual patient.)

The other analogy I would like to offer is of the feelings being like molten bronze, having no form until they are poured into a mould or cast. Then we can see the form of an otter, Napoleon, or an abstract design. In this analogy, the mould is the patient. Only when the analyst's feelings have taken on the shape of the mould can he *feel* the patient. It may help us in our discussion if we call feelings with a definable form just feelings, and feelings in the amorphous state, proto-feelings.

The transformation of proto-feelings into feelings takes a long time. It may take months or years. I used to say to people I supervised at the Tavistock that, in a year of very fruitful psychotherapy with a patient, you would be lucky if there were six true interpretations. The analyst's role then is not to let the conversation prevent those six interpretations from emerging. I was once told of a girl who played the French horn in an orchestra. On one particular night she had only one note to play in the entire concert. At the precise moment she was due to play it, she was distracted by seeing her boyfriend come into the concert hall and so missed it.

Although I have said that the mould is the patient, this is not strictly accurate. The moulder of the feelings is the relationship between the patient and the analyst, of which the conversation is the symbolic expression. It is this that effectively transforms proto-feelings into feelings. The conversation that goes on between patient and analyst is the medium of exchange, as it was in the case I quoted earlier about the girl whose three grandparents had committed suicide. That conversation had enabled my feeling about her to emerge. In other words, the transformation of proto-feeling into feeling had taken place. (Social conversations are normally constructed to prevent such transformations; regrettably, psychoanalytic conversations also frequently block them.)

The process of waiting is very difficult for human beings. I am not sure why this is, but from my own experience, from listening to clinical presentations, and from supervising, I know it comes hard. The temptation to collude with the psychotic's fantasy is very great. It is difficult for an analyst to be the servant of the process instead of its master. To have mastered a theory in terms of which everything is understood gives a feeling of power—it is rather like the power a man might feel if he were driving a Ferrari at 150 miles an hour along the highway. To renounce this power and instead put our faith in something much more uncertain, much less trustworthy, may seem to be pure folly. Yet I believe that the psychoanalytic process demands just this of us.

The burden of unbearable feelings

The second obstacle in reaching his own feelings is the presence in the analyst of unbearable feelings. When a patient approaches an analyst, he always has some feelings that he asks the analyst to bear. The analyst is only able to do this if he feels comfortable with such feelings. What I am talking about now is something over and above the difficulties of transforming proto-feelings into feelings. Certain configurations of proto-feelings press for transformation, but the ego is not able to bear them.

- I was once treating a devout Christian. He found it unbearable to consider that in his motivations he was thoroughly self-centred.

- A woman I was once treating led on the surface a very glamorous life. She had had an unbelievable range of adventures and many interesting friends, and she was widely travelled. But she was escaping. One day she had a dream and in it she was sitting beside a black coffin. This deathly depression became unbearable, and she came into analysis because in her saner moments she wanted to begin to bear that black coffin.

- For another patient, it was a great inner loneliness; for yet another, a crushing disappointment; and in another, a vicious envy that covered a deeply felt sense of being psychologically deformed.

It is the analyst's task to help the patient bear these feelings, to be there with the patient. But if the analyst also has feelings that he cannot bear, he will repudiate those same feelings in the patient. He will do this unconsciously. It is when these proto-feelings in the analyst have not reached the status of feelings, and no transformation has occurred, that there is trouble.

I said earlier that the relationship between two people expressed in their conversation was the medium of transformation. This is true, but there is also another element. It is frequently observable that a person starts off in analysis unable to bear certain feelings or certain truths. When the situation changes and he is able to bear them, it means that the capacity was there but it needed to be brought to birth. This occurred through the belief of another, something that happens through the analytic process. The coming to birth of the innate capacity and the growth of belief go hand in hand—photosynthesis cannot occur without sunlight.

Psychotic transference

While the difficulties inherent in the transformation of proto-feelings into feelings are germane to all human encounters, and the specific difficulties that can arise if the same area of truth is unbearable to both parties are characteristic of neurosis, a further set of difficulties to beset the analyst's feelings arises in the case of psychosis.

In the case of a neurotic transference, a few similarities between the behaviour of the analyst, however tenuous, and the intrapsychic object (made up of memory and phantasy) allow a projection of this inner object onto the analyst. The patient perceives the analyst to be behaving *like* his mother or father, or brother or sister. In a psychotic transference, however, the analyst is believed to *be* the patient's mother or father, or brother or sister. I well remember how taken aback I was when I realized that a patient thought I *was* his mother. On another occasion, a girl thought I was her boyfriend. In such a transference, the analyst is totally fused with another figure.

But it is not only that the analyst is fused with another important figure in the patient's life, but also that the patient is fused with the analyst. The patient does not know what is he and what is the analyst. He does not know whether a feeling belongs to him or whether it is the analyst's feeling. The only way in which such a transference can be resolved is for the analyst to take ownership of his own feelings. Only then can the patient find his own feelings and separate out from the analyst. "Tell me who you are," says the patient, "and then I can find myself."

This may sound an easy task, but it is in fact one of extreme difficulty and one whereby the analyst will have to pass through flood-tides of anxiety. In a psychotic transference, neither analyst nor patient knows what is he and what is the other. Such fusion takes place through powerful projective, introjective, and regressive forces, yet in the midst of these great emotional storms the analyst must find his own feelings. If he manages to do it, the patient can grow and the analyst will grow mentally, too.

The realities of the analyst's work

I have briefly outlined the difficulties for the analyst in reaching his own feelings in normal, neurotic, and psychotic encounters. Human encounters are not, however, divided tidily into one or another of these. In normal encounters, there will be elements of neurotic phenomena and even traces of psychotic processes. In a neurotic transference, there will be normal elements and psychotic elements, and in a psychotic transference there will be neurotic as well as normal elements. In all these cases, the reaching of one's own feelings is therapeutic for both patient and analyst.

The inner task is a life's work

One of the most moving personal accounts within recent psychoanalytic literature must be Guntrip's narrative of his two analyses with Fairbairn and Winnicott. In his account, Guntrip (1975) tells us how it was only at the end of a long life that he reached down to his deepest feelings. Shortly before he died, he had two dreams where he found himself back with "the 'faceless' depersonalized mother" and "the black depressed mother, who totally failed to relate" (pp. 145–146).

In his first analysis with Fairbairn, he worked through powerful negative feelings towards his dominant attacking mother. With

Winnicott, he reached back to his mother's "paralysing schizoid aloofness". The dominance and the hostility in him and in his mother had ultimately been a defence against an appalling black hole of depression. Shortly before his death, Winnicott analysed Guntrip, which enabled Guntrip subsequently to reach back to the emptiness of those early feelings. It is clear from the account that Winnicott had himself managed to reach his own deeper feelings, that a transformation of proto-feelings into feelings had become possible. At one point, after making an interpretation to Guntrip, Winnicott said: "I couldn't have made that interpretation five years ago."

This transforming process is a psychic work that lasts the whole of a person's lifetime. Guntrip and Winnicott were both sensitive analysts, and yet, from that account, it is clear that their growth in capacity to interpret to their patients was in accordance with the transforming psychic activity in their own inner lives. Whether a patient ever meets up with the right analyst and whether that patient meets that analyst at the "peak" moment of his life is very much in the lap of the gods. If such a meeting does occur, it is one of life's moments of good fortune.

Conclusion

The analyst's task is to reach his own feelings. These feelings are partly modelled by the patient who is in interaction with him. This happens through a communication system that occurs at the sensational level of experience. To reach his own feelings means pain and loneliness. If, however, he reaches his own feelings, it frees the patient and favours his emotional development. This inner task is a life's work for the analyst.

CHAPTER FOUR

Imagination
and curiosity of mind

This chapter is based on two papers, one entitled "The Imagination required in our Environment" and the other "Curiosity of Mind". These topics are here linked together: both are states of mind that I believe have equal value, imagination being the producer of creative thought and feelings, and curiosity being a mental attitude. The previous chapter dealt with the importance of a psychotherapist being guided by his feelings. What I want to explore further are those elements that transform proto-feelings into feelings—elements that are intrinsic parts of the mental structure that forms personality. These elements are closely interwoven with feelings and, like feelings, can be developed through education. For a student of psychotherapy, two of the most important transforming elements are, I believe, the imagination and curiosity of mind.

Imagination is the psychotherapist's instrument of understanding. It may sound strange to say this, but I think it is true that it is through the imagination that one human being makes contact with another, and through the imagination that the psychotherapist makes emotional contact with the patient. It is the mental faculty the psychotherapist most needs to cultivate, after such character traits as integrity and trustworthiness.

The nature of imagination

I want to start by making the following surprising statement: it is possible to alter our past lives through the imagination. This applies notwithstanding the fact that it contradicts the practical man who says, "What is done is done, what has happened has happened." After all, if I look back on my life, there are certain established facts that history cannot change or rewrite. That is the position that is taken by the scientific rationalist—scientific facts are immutable states of affair. This view of a fact, that it is solid and cannot be moved, is in no way conditioned by relation to other facts. There is no sense in it because it derives its factuality in its relationship to other facts. An example might be a landscape painting focusing on a tree whose trunk is the darkest object within the field of the painter's vision. The only way that it receives its quality of darkness is through its relation to other objects in the painting which are lighter.

The same thing is true of all the so-called solid facts of our lives. There are certain things that are unchangeable. For instance, the facts that John Smith was born on 5 January 1951 and that Murphy was 5 foot 2 inches in height will not be changed, nor will the fact that one person was born and another will one day die, and so on. However, there are other kinds of facts, like when someone tells me that their mother was cruel to them, their father treated them unfairly, or they hate their brother. These sorts of facts obtain their factual quality from what a sociologist would call the domain assumptions that a person has.

Domain assumptions

A domain assumption is an all-pervading and deeply rooted attitude to life, which is rooted in the unconscious and not only colours the events, happenings, and relationships of a person's life, but also invests those events with a certain character, so that the person who said that his mother was cruel might also have said that he was unfairly treated at work, have formed a cynical attitude towards politics, and so on. Domain assumptions cover the way that a person actually experiences their primary relationships. When someone says his mother was cruel to him, he might be able to produce facts to prove it, but it could also fall from a domain assumption that the individual is always the victim of society.

These so-called solid facts of people's lives are always psychologically determined; the determining occurrences are rooted in the domain assumptions that inhabit a part of the personality of which, except in rare moments, the subject is unconscious. In psychoanalytic literature it is described as the psychotic area of the personality. This point can be illustrated by the case of the patient I described in the previous chapter who complained that her colleagues at work were always exploiting her, and who subsequently experienced a gradual and pleasant shift in attitudes towards her. The very facts of her life, the facts that seemed to be static, ineradicable entities, had actually changed, and a crucial factor in this change was the psychotherapist's imagination. My imagination had been instrumental in making my perception, my inner psychic registration of her, alter.

Absence of imagination

I once had a patient who came to me following a serious psychotic breakdown. Her communications were "telegraphic bits": she would say something like "Smile of the Cheshire Cat", there would be a silence, and then she would say "Yellow", and so on. I found myself weaving these discrete images (which I later realized were hallucinatory objects that she was seeing in my consulting-room) into a fantastic and weird pattern—a pattern that was, I came to realize, the elemental work of the imagination.

It seems that, if the imagination ceases to function, we get a state of affairs such as the one occurring in my patient. When the world is a chaos of sensations coming from within our own psychic structure and also from external sources, we cannot link them together into a meaningful whole without the creative faculty of imagination. In fact, this patient had held herself together through a very rigid political ideology to which she clung, plus a job that was principally concerned with statistics for demographic purposes. This patient's breakdown, then, revealed a total absence of a functional imagination, and my response had been to offer her the use of my own imagination until such time as she had sufficient confidence in herself to begin to use her own.

In fact, things are not quite as simple as that, because if there has never been an imagination, an internal picture-making, pattern-making faculty, there is just chaos. The imagination has to start externally. It is significant, I think, that this patient for the first time in her life began to draw and paint pictures. She felt it to be absolutely necessary. I think that, for her, it was part of the process of bringing an inchoate imagination into being. This is the reason why in most schools today children are encouraged enormously to draw and paint. Bettelheim says in his book, *The Uses of Enchantment* (1977), that it is a great mistake for books of fairy tales to be illustrated because, he believes, it is better for children to create their own images of the story. Where neither person has imagination, the patient clings to a belief, to an ideology, or to anecdotal principles, and the psychotherapist clings to a theory. In other words, it is possible to have, in the consulting-rooms, two robots reacting to each other. It is only when the imagination functions that the two robots can become two people. My central point is that it is through the imagination that the meaningful world as we know it is constructed.

In a sense, it is true to say that patients come to see us when things have broken down and when their lives no longer hold meaning for them: they place implicit trust in the psychotherapist's ability to help them rebuild their world. Unless the imagination of the psychotherapist is in a healthy, functioning state, he cannot help them construct the new meaningful world they so desperately need.

The relation of imagination to feelings

The psychotherapist has to be guided by his feelings. What he decides to select for interpretation, out of the many things the patient tells him, is governed by his feelings. This is even so when the psychotherapist is under supervision. If the supervisor tells the psychotherapist to say something with which he feels uncomfortable, then it is those feelings of discomfort that are his guide. If he overrides his feelings out of a sense of loyalty to a supervisor, then he is betraying both himself and his patient (and also the supervisor).

I will not go further here into the subject of feelings, but I do want to dwell on what it is in the personality that transforms proto-feelings into feelings (a subject covered in chapter three). I believe that this transformer is the imagination. At any one moment in time, we are bombarded by tactile sensations and other stimuli, both internal and external, which do not as yet have the quality of feelings. The imagination takes up this raw material and transforms it into patterned imagery so that a feeling comes into being. The feeling comes into being through the imaginative processes in the mind.

Towards a better understanding

But where do the psychotherapist's images come from? I think one of the tragedies of many training courses is that a particular model, or even perhaps two or three, are offered to trainees, according to which they are to understand and interpret the communications of their patients. However, this is enormously reductionist. There is also no guarantee that these models in any way correspond to the psychotherapist's own personal life and experience.

So, to start with, I think any trainee psychotherapist needs at his disposal a good grounding in theoretical models, as described in chapter two, where I discussed the Academic Model. But, much more importantly, due to the acknowledged deficiencies of that model, he also needs to have available a whole range of images arising from his own present and past life, stretching right back to his childhood, in order to meet the stimuli, sensations, and sensuous modalities that come to him when he is sitting with a patient.

A store of mental images

The richer the memory store of images available to the therapist, the greater is his chance of being able to make a fortuitous construction. It is important that the psychotherapist should freely exercise his imagination while in the process of determining the most appropriate treatment programme for the patient. If, at the initial assessment interview, the patient is allowed to talk freely and the psychotherapist relaxes into an inner attitude of free association, the latter's own fantasy life will frequently lead him to the area in which the patient has the greatest difficulty.

Imagine a painter going down to the harbour in order to do a waterscape of the scene that confronts him. He surveys the scene, then he starts to paint; the water is looking dapple-green, and the sky is varied with a few bits of blue. But a few minutes later that same water may be dark and the sky overcast. Monet was so fascinated with this phenomenon that on one occasion he was working on 200 canvases simultaneously. Moving from canvas to canvas, he took in on each canvas the scene as it was at that moment: a different image was necessary from one moment to the next. It is one of the defects of the intellect (as the French philosopher Henri Bergson has pointed out) that it can only conceptualize the static, whereas feelings change from moment to moment as does the scene in front of the painter. And, as the feelings change, so also will the image. Therefore, if the psychotherapist is to stay in touch with his patient—as that patient is at that particular moment—he must be able freely to draw on his own personal memory bank of images. Of all the recognized models that are presented to trainee psychotherapists in order that they may understand their patients, I have yet to find the patient who exactly fits any of them.

Making myths

When the psychotherapist stays in touch with his patient, they are together making a new construction, creating a new imaginative universe, or, quite simply, making a myth.

> I had a patient once whose mother, it seemed, had greeted his birth with enormous enthusiasm—she was charmed by this new, beautiful, golden-haired baby. However, when she found that this baby shitted and urinated, she handed him to her own mother to look after.

> When he came to see me, he went to great efforts to make sure that he was no trouble at all. He had the feeling that if he were in any way a trouble or a nuisance or, in other words, a shitty baby, I would drop him and send him off to another psycho-therapist. It was through my consultations with him and from various things he told me about his mother, his grandmother, and his early childhood that we made a reconstruction. When she discovered that her golden-haired baby had an unfortu-nate propensity to shit and urinate and vomit, she dropped him. This, anyway, was the construction that he and I made. It may not have been the exact reason his mother dropped him. It was a myth that for him and for me made sense of a certain pattern of behaviour that led him to be used as a doormat in his professional career.

Through the imagination, the psychotherapist and patient create a myth, and it is this mutual myth-making that is healing.

Philosophers, psychotherapists, and imagination

The philosopher David Hume thought that the mind functioned through a process of association of one thing to another. He be-lieved, therefore, that imagination was extremely limited and could do nothing to alter the streams of associated facts that con-fronted the mind. At the other end of the spectrum was the twentieth-century philosopher John Paul Sartre, who believed that the imagination was totally free of any necessity, that the imagination creates something out of nothing.

The philosopher Kant distinguished between empirical imagination and transcendental imagination. The former, he said, unifies impressions and enables a particular object to be named and recognized, but it is essentially passive and therefore subject to incoming impressions. This was the imagination as David Hume understood it, but Kant also said that there was a transcendental imagination which has a constructive function that is active and has a spontaneous power. I am not sure how valuable this distinction is except perhaps to recognize that imagination has a wide-ranging set of functions within the human mind. I think it is probable that both David Hume and John Paul Sartre are in error and that the truth lies somewhere midway between the two. In this light, then, I think that the myth I constructed with the golden-haired patient would not have worked if it had had no real material to give substance to it. So, too, a piece of factual or biographical reconstruction on its own would be a purposeless exercise.

When Freud started psychoanalysis, he was working within the traditions of David Hume, James Mill, and others. He followed the associative links between one thing that a patient said and another. However, I think that very few psychotherapists today try to understand the patient by slavishly associating one chunk of communication with another. What this fails to do justice to is the uniqueness of human communication. It may (although I doubt it) do justice to our perceptual reconstruction of the non-human universe, but it certainly does not do justice to an understanding of another *person*. I believe that the deepest contact between one human being and another occurs through shared fantasy life in the unconscious. Therefore, within psychoanalysis, I think there has been a very radical departure from the old analytic method following the introduction of countertransference by Winnicott (1947) and Paula Heimann (1950)—because what Winnicott was saying, which was then more fully elaborated by Paula Heimann, was that the psychotherapist needs to attend not just to the associations of the patient, but also to the patterning of his own feelings.

Educating the imagination

Many trainee psychotherapists first undergo training as medical doctors. That is a particular route that I myself have not travelled, but I understand that the training is very technical and lacks subjects like history, literature, anthropology, and so on (I am not sure that psychologists or social workers have done much better). Quite how doctors came therefore to be in charge of this world, which supremely demands the exercise of the imagination, seems to be due to a series of historical accidents.

Since an integral part of the psychotherapist's education should be the cultivation of the imagination, we need to consider what kind of culture it is that promotes the flights of imagination that are so essential if psychotherapy is to be successful. It is possible to be with a patient who fosters the psychotherapist's imagination; it is also possible to be with a patient who throttles our imaginative processes. You can divide psychotherapists into two groups: those who truly believe that a patient can affect even such internal processes in the mind, and those who do not. I belong to the former group. In addition, there are certain mental and environmental factors that influence the proper cultivation and fostering of the imagination.

The psychotherapeutic culture

Just as it is possible for two different patients to have such different effects on us, so also can the culture in which psychotherapy takes place have the same differential. I have worked as a psychotherapist in a culture in which there was so much envy, rivalry, and splitting that my anxiety reached a level where it was not possible for my imagination to work. I have also worked in a setting that enormously favoured imaginative conjecture. I would particularly select envy as being one of the great enemies of the imagination. I think Melanie Klein (1957) was right when she said that individual creativity, especially, is an object of envious attack. The envious person cannot bear the creative or imaginative searchings of another.

I also agree with Melanie Klein when she said that within the one individual there can be a stifling of the creative impulses through the presence within the psychic structure of an envious figure. There can be a complex within the personality that seizes upon the first signs of individual and personal imagination. I have often had the experience of patients who transfer this on to the psychotherapist and thereby become terrified of his envy. This is also so within a psychotherapeutic culture. The tendency, for instance, to institutionalize a new idea before it has had a chance to grow and develop is a typical device for strangling imaginative processes. So also is the insistence on a monolithic system that strangles freedom. Imagination and freedom, as Sartre has emphasized, are bedfellows—in fact, Sartre believed that imagination was *the* agency within the personality that guaranteed freedom. In terms of a culture—a training environment—that encourages the imagination and curiosity of mind, I would say the most important hallmarks are receptivity, non-defensiveness, and tolerance. In a superego culture, the imagination becomes crippled, and, unfortunately, such cultures are common within psychotherapy communities.

Mental space

Freud did not bring up this topic of imagination and curiosity directly, but he implied it when he said: "Experience soon showed that the attitude which the analytic physician could most advantageously adopt was to surrender himself to his own unconscious mental activity, in a state of evenly suspended attention, to avoid so far as possible reflection and the construction of conscious expectations" (1923a, p. 239). This is not exactly the same as imagination, but he is talking about the mental conditions necessary for the imagination to operate to its maximum capacity. Just as muscles soon degenerate if they are not used, so does the imagination. It is not only through use that the imagination is actualized; it also requires a certain mental culture. The central ingredient of this culture is mental space.

I remember at university a lecturer in English literature saying that he hoped none of his students had mortgages, because if they had, it would interfere with the free exercise of their imaginative exploration. He also meant that this faculty needs to be fed—after all, it is the faculty that reconstructs not only the images that are present to us in the here and now, but also all the images of a lifetime that lie in the conscious and unconscious memory. The contemplation of the natural landscape and of works of art, listening to music, and the enjoyment of poetry are all food for the soul and for the imagination. If mental space is a prerequisite for the healthy functioning of the imagination, then the timetable needs to reflect this. The work of the imagination requires great mental effort—usually it is much easier to rush off and clutch at a passing theory. But when we do this, we give up on that struggle to stay in emotional contact with our patients. The imagination will thrive if it is given unrestricted mental space and a conducive environment.

The physical environment

There is an additional aspect to the type of environment conducive to the free exercise of the imagination, and that is the physical one. The interior decoration of the psychotherapy rooms and the whole psychotherapy department will, in itself, play an important part in both the activity of psychotherapy and the enjoyment of the results. For I believe that if we really take the cultivation of the imagination seriously, then within the educational programme there needs to be time put aside for such subjects, normally included under the title of the fine arts. I believe that it is a source of considerable deprivation that psychotherapy and even psychotherapy training is conducted within the concrete jungle that usually makes up a university campus. Such an environment can only foster mental delinquency. I believe that to some extent the psychotherapist, as an individual, needs to feel at home in his room so that it has some personal associations for him. He needs to be rooted in his own self and not shorn of all personal elements.

Curiosity of mind

The question to which a lifetime in the profession seeks an answer is, "How does the mind work?" It would therefore be pointless for someone to wish to become a psychotherapist unless their natural disposition and orientation of interest inclined them to be curious about the workings of the mind. However, one does not necessarily pursue that interest by becoming a psychotherapist. After all, someone might study philosophy and psychology and receive thereby a very comprehensive understanding of the mind. So, what is it about the psychotherapeutic procedure that is different from pursuing this knowledge either as a philosopher or as an academic psychologist?

Of the two spheres of a person's life—the emotional sphere that is generated by close intimate relations with other people and the intellectual, cognitive sphere that is exercised through work— it is on the emotional sphere that the psychotherapist's interest is mostly focused. That is not to say, of course, that the two spheres are separate—emotional factors frequently obstruct a person's capacity for work. I have witnessed on many occasions a person whose work as a surgeon, a lawyer, an insurance broker, a doctor, a painter, a writer, or an accountant has been enhanced and considerably developed as a result of the removal of those obstructive emotional elements. The curious mind will want to know why— what is the interconnection between the emotional event and the capacity to be a better surgeon, lawyer, doctor, painter, or whatever? The curious mind will want to have a grasp of both these interconnections and of the different levels of functioning within the personality.

The dangers of an incurious mind

What are the consequences if a psychotherapist does not have this innate interest in the working of the mind? I said in the Introduction to the book that what differentiated psychotherapy from psychoanalysis was that the former's goal was cure, whereas the latter's was understanding and self-understanding of the mind. Is it all right, then, if the psychotherapist notes that, with the removal of an emotional obstruction, there is an improvement in mental stamina and is then satisfied with that and looks no further into it? I think one needs to note that this is an attitude that is not essentially different from that of a behavioural kind of therapy. I do not say this in order to denigrate behavioural therapy, but to point out that a psychotherapist who is operating in this way is partly using a behavioural model.

This analogy can be carried further, because without curiosity of mind the psychotherapist will be making use of certain models or theories he has learned during his training which then become applied to the material that the patient presents. It may be effective, but there is no guarantee that these theories will correlate with the inner workings of the patient's mind. It means that the therapeutic cure is always in danger of having been effected through the patient's deep desire to please the psychotherapist— narcissistic patients, in particular, are capable of producing the sort of material that the psychotherapist wants to hear. In such cases, then, the cure is an outer compliance, and, although it may look as if it is heartfelt, time nearly always reveals that the true state of affairs is quite different. However, if the psychotherapist had an innate interest in the working of the mind, this interest would function as a buffer against cures based on compliance of this nature.

There is another aspect to this as well, and that is the psychotherapist's own personal response in relation to his patient. As I said in chapter two, concerning the psychotherapist's education, unless interpretations issue from the psychotherapist's own core convictions they are not effective. Without curiosity of mind, it is impossible that the package of theories which the psychotherapist has to rely upon is a true echo of his own inner personal self.

Developing curiosity of mind
in the trainee psychotherapist

Although it is an innate part of the personality, I think that curiosity can be developed a great deal. An educational programme that is exceedingly wide-ranging should provide the opportunities for such development. Again, in chapter two, I wrote how an important insight came to me while reading George Eliot's *Middlemarch*, but that insight would not have come unless I had been searching for the solution to a problem.

This brings me to another kind of point. As soon as you begin to think about the mind and how it works, and the first fumbling hypotheses begin to develop, you are confronted with one problem after another after another. These problems are not always articulated consciously, or, at least, they may be articulated consciously for a time and then they go underground again. But even when they go below the threshold of awareness, they remain as inner searchings or what Wilfrid Bion called "preconceptions". As soon as one problem has been solved, it becomes the starting point for a new one. This search never finishes—it goes on and on and we can never reach a point where we can sit back and say, "Now we have solved it". There is another great advantage in the adoption of this attitude of mind, and this is a therapeutic one. The patient in a process like this will always be contributing to the evolving model. The very fact of this psychic and emotional contribution builds a strength into the inner structure of the ego.

I believe that a great many psychotherapy training programmes that try to instil a particular model of the mind often do so at the expense of the personal development of the trainee psychotherapist. There is one maxim that can be adhered to quite safely: any psychotherapy system that is easy to teach and can be mastered quickly has to be based on an abortion of the truth. Such systems are an insult to those great spirits in human history who have charted with courage the avenues of thought in the human mind. It may be obvious and it may seem that it is not necessary to say this, but in the last ten years I have seen so many "get-rich-quick" approaches to the psychotherapeutic endeavour that I feel it necessary to point out how misleading such activities are. I do not expect that it will ever be possible to deter the missionary figures from preaching their different messages, but I think it might be possible to sow a seed of doubt in those whom they lead astray.

Conclusion

A personal understanding of the human world, and, in particular, of the workings of the human mind, cannot be achieved without the discoveries and inevitably painful insights that accompany emotional curiosity. Curiosity of mind, I believe, is a quality that is essential for this vocation, and it is not possible for someone to be a safe psychotherapist unless they have this quality, this interest, as a guiding light in their work. Development of the imagination is, I believe, equally crucial in the making of a psychotherapist. I think Bion (1978) was trying to get at this once in a seminar when he said: "When you have seen a patient, instead of going and writing up the session, why not instead go and make a painting of the next session."

CHAPTER FIVE

Mental pain and moral courage

T his chapter is based on two papers, one entitled "Pain" and the other "Moral Courage". I have already touched upon mental suffering in my discussion of the Invention Model of education and in the conclusion to the previous chapter—it is, in fact, inevitably touched upon many times. And, because I believe that no psychotherapist can be effective unless he can reach his own feelings, moral fortitude is an essential quality in a psychotherapist if he is to endure the pain that reaching those feelings entails. In other words, moral courage is needed to deal with mental pain.

It is a universal truth that all animals seek to avoid pain, and mankind is no exception to this general principle. Human beings have found the means to relieve physical pain, so that today we have extremely effective drugs that can prevent the patient from being exposed to the full intensity of certain illnesses. In addition, the duration of these illnesses is often very much reduced. It also seems to be the case that a person's health benefits from this alleviation of pain. There does not seem to be any accompanying constituent to physical pain that is essential for the physical well-being of the organism.

Just as there is physical pain, so also there is mental pain, and, in exactly the same way that we shrink from the former, it is our natural tendency to avoid the latter. There is, however, this big difference between physical pain and mental pain at the present stage in our knowledge of mental and emotional life. It is that emotional and mental development cannot occur without pain. Therefore, the person who resolutely sets his face against the possibility of suffering pain is condemned to remain in a state of emotional childhood. Freud named this desire to repudiate mental pain "resistance". He said that it is a very strange thing that someone will decide to go into psychoanalysis at great financial expense and also at great cost in terms of time and commitment, and yet, when he arrives in the consulting-room, he starts trying to resist the analyst's attempts to treat him.

> When I was living and working in London, I once had a patient who lived just outside Birmingham who got up at 4 a.m. to drive to London, a two-hour journey. He arrived shortly after 6 a.m., left me at 7 a.m. and drove back to Birmingham in order to arrive at his office in time for work. He did this twice a week. This occurred shortly after I qualified as a psychoanalyst, and I somehow thought that, with all the effort he was making, surely there would be no resistance. Of course, I was being absurd. He tried to resist the mental pain to which he was exposed just as surely as someone tries to resist the pain when a dentist drills into a nerve without an anaesthetic.

The psychotherapist is constantly up against patients who want to be cured but, at the same time, do everything in their power to avoid mental pain. The patient will develop every kind of subtle device to try to persuade the psychotherapist to steer away from the area of pain. The psychotherapist will be greatly tempted to go along with this because he himself, being human, will also want to avoid pain.

The nature of mental pain

A good way to examine the nature of mental pain is through case studies.

> I was once treating a mentally handicapped man who was aged 33. As the therapy progressed, it became evident to me that he exaggerated, both in his own mind and also in his presentation of himself to others, the degree of his mental handicap. Then, as this started to become evident to him, possibilities that had not seemed to be present before began to open up to him. The result of this was that he began to feel that most of his life had been wasted. This realization was exceedingly painful to him.

I can think of many cases where a realization has caused the patient great mental distress:

> • A girl I was once treating came to the realization that she had never loved anyone; another patient finally faced the painful fact that her mother did not love her; another had filled her life with exciting events in order to protect herself from a massive black depression.

> • A man I was once treating came to realize that he had missed out on some very basic experiences of being loved and nurtured by his parents. In addition to the pain of feeling that he had missed out on this, he had felt a terrible shame in relation to his peers at school and later to his friends and to his peers at work.

This leads me into the area with which all psychotherapists are familiar: the very painful early experiences that are encoded within the personality but which each one of us strenuously avoids re-experiencing. So, instead of experiencing the pain ourselves, we dramatize it within the social environment in which we live. In other words, our social environment becomes a stage on which we project pain that we are unable to bear.

Identifying a common denominator

Is there any common denominator that makes sense of all these diverse instances of mental pain? What is the element common to all of them? I think that mental pain is the subjective experience of deficiency in the self. If someone is unable to love, it is a deficiency of the self which is perhaps even more painful than being blind. Perhaps a better term than "deficiency of the self" would be "self-diminishment". All those factors or life events that diminish us are subjectively experienced as pain. The source of this diminishment can be from within ourselves or can be caused by factors in our social environment. I think that the pain is always concerned with those ways in which we ourselves have contributed to our diminishment.

The case of the mentally handicapped man is something that will always stay in my mind for this reason. When he began to realize that he had constructed his life around an illusion and that he had been in a prison that had seriously restricted him, he began to cry. I have often been in the presence of people who have cried, but never in my life have I ever come across crying like that. It came from the very depth of him: he was in such intense pain that I found it almost unbearable to be in the same room with him. It was deeply upsetting to be in the presence of someone who was so deeply distressed, and I have no doubt that his distress touched areas in me that were unspeakably painful. I believe that this is why it is extremely difficult for one human being to stay with another who is in a state of severe distress—it is a social situation we usually try to avoid. We make reassuring noises and say that it will probably be all right or that perhaps it will be better next time, or make some absurdly trivial remark to try to alleviate the agony.

So we avoid mental pain in others because it is so painful to ourselves—it brings us nakedly face to face with our own diminishments. Therefore, in the psychotherapeutic situation there is not just one person, the patient, who is wanting to avoid pain, but two. A colleague of mine in London used to say, "The difficulty with psychoanalysis is that even the analyst is against it". Yet the paradox is that an individual can bear mental pain only if there is someone there able to bear it with him. Fundamentally, it is not a question of saying the right thing but of being conscious of the pain in the other person, and not saying anything that will save us and the patient from experiencing it.

Masochism

The person who is masochistic inflicts pain on himself.

> I once had a patient who told me how bad, how unworthy she was. She slaved away all day, worked overtime in her job, and was extremely submissive to her very authoritarian husband. She was constantly saying what an awful person she was, yet she gave out an air of self-sacrifice. One day, she told me a lie and I challenged her with it. She was absolutely furious. She told me how virtuous she was, how respected she was, that no one else had ever said such a thing to her, and so on. What emerged was that her masochistic stance was a barrier she had erected in order to prevent me getting near her and, in fact, to prevent me from pointing out things to her that were truly painful.

I believe that masochism is the self-infliction of pain, and its purpose is to prevent the experience of true pain.

The need for emotional strength

Most of us use the word "emotional" a great deal, but its meaning is usually vague. If we say that someone is physically strong, we are saying that he is able to exert a pressure of above average pounds per square inch. But what do we mean when we say that someone is emotionally strong? A person who is emotionally strong, we believe, is able to withstand the pressure of projective identification to a degree that is above average.

The meaning of projective identification

The following imaginary scenario will illustrate what is meant by the term "projective identification".

> Five policemen were conversing in a local police station. Although they did not have definite evidence, they were sure that two recent burglaries that had taken place within their area had been done by an old-timer called Jimmy Tolbine. They therefore decided to arrest him and bring him in for questioning. However, they made a sort of pact among themselves that they would not accept any of his protests and lies to the effect that he was not the culprit. So they arrested Tolbine and started questioning him, amid cynical smiles all round.
>
> However, one policeman, Joe Smith, began to have doubts as to Tolbine's guilt, since some of Tolbine's responses to his questions sounded convincing. A little later, the policeman in charge of the investigation said to Tolbine, "Well, Jimmy Tolbine, we are going to put you on charges because we have evidence that you are guilty", and then he looked around at the faces of his four colleagues. His expression held quite a menacing glare. Although Joe Smith had his doubts, he felt full of fear at giving voice to them. The policeman in charge was speaking in leering and cynical terms, and the other policemen were all nodding assent to what he said. Smith found himself quailing inside.

This is the kind of moment when emotional courage is required. The pressure, silent but exceedingly powerful, that was put upon Joe Smith by the other police, the dilemma that he felt, and the quailing feeling that he experienced are what is meant by projective identification. The group projected into Smith threats lest he do anything but concur with them. The threats are not verbal—they are conveyed through non-verbal cues. It was Melanie Klein who first identified this emotional phenomenon and gave it its name.

It is probably quite possible to divide psychotherapists into those who "believe" in projective identification and those who do not. I put the word "believe" in inverted commas because this is not a correct description. A lot of people know, for instance, what we mean when we use the word "fear", although I once met a man who said he could not imagine how it was possible to feel fear, except on the field of battle when the shells were exploding all around. Most of us, however, have experienced fear in many situations other than the one cited. Many people experience fear in social situations. It is very common for someone to experience fear before making an address to a large audience, and it is quite common for someone to have fear when they must personally deliver an unpleasant piece of news. Fear of this sort is often referred to as anxiety. Fear, then, is an inner psychic reality which does have external concomitants. Projective identification is a reality of this nature. It has an inner component and an outer component.

Projective identification as an emotional phenomenon

In the example I gave of Joe Smith, he felt fear—he felt that if he spoke and gave voice to his doubts, he would suffer pain. He experienced himself as being in danger; this feeling emanated from something real that was intimated in the personalities of the other policemen. What I am saying, therefore, is that projective identification is not a theory, it is an emotional phenomenon. This phenomenon is frequently present in a very high degree of intensity in the consulting-room. For instance, the psychotherapist may feel that to make certain interpretations would be too painful.

A psychotherapist once shirked saying to a patient that what he was saying only made sense on the assumption that the patient was very dependent upon the approval of others, and without it could hardly get along in social life. When questioned as to why he had not been able to say it, the psychotherapist replied that it was such an integral part of the patient's self-image—that he was independent—that he felt it would be too much of a blow to him to make the interpretation that had presented itself to him. It became apparent from other clinical presentations that this patient put out a very powerful message, which said, "I am very vulnerable—please don't hurt me".

It takes emotional courage on the part of the psychotherapist to persevere and say what is true. I have called this requirement courage because I think this is what it is normally called in common conversation. It is usually referred to as moral courage as opposed to physical courage. But we need to look a bit more closely at the inner situation. It is clear from the clinical practice of psychoanalysis that, when there is an inhibition against speaking, it betrays the presence of a bullying tyrant within. There emerges a constellation, which is that part of the personality which might be called the emotional child, being terrorized by a very hostile presence within. There is, then, within, a tyrant and a frightened child. This tyrant is more than can be borne by the patient, and he finds it intolerable even to contemplate being the possessor of such a presence. It is, we believe, itself made up of many different elements. These elements, in part or as a whole, are violently disowned, and in that process they become lodged in the other person or persons. It may not happen in this way, just as we do not know exactly how a fear is imparted in such a way that an individual experiences it in a social situation—all we know is that such a fear is experienced. And what we are sure of is that this fear, in a social situation, is the product of a pressure that we call projective identification.

What is certain is that there is a very big difference between those psychotherapists who say that such a phenomenon is insignificant and not something of which a psychotherapist need take note, and the psychotherapist who says that this phenomenon is extremely important and that if it is ignored there will not be any lasting cure. I have always believed that projective identification is too important for the psychotherapist to ignore. In whatever form it takes, there is always one common denominator in the therapeutic situation. It erects a barrier to stop the psychotherapist giving support to the emotional creative self at the core of the personality. This creative core has often lacked the force and strength that are needed to become active and present in the personality in such a way that it permeates and gives colour to the person's emotional, artistic, or scientific life. Psychotherapists who are very antagonistic to the idea of taking seriously the interactive process of projective identification often believe that it leads to a persecuting style of therapy. It is true that this sometimes happens. But that criticism misses the whole point, which is that the purpose of transforming a projective identification into linguistic communication is to free the patient's creative positive capacities. There is one thing that is certain: that where projective identification is powerful, love and creativity are, to that extent, smothered. As love is inhibited by fear, so too is creativity smothered by projective identification.

The demand, therefore, for moral courage in the psychotherapist is an invitation to grow emotionally. When the patient and the psychotherapist start off in a joint endeavour, they have made an agreement to embrace emotional growth. The presence of projective identification, of which the psychotherapist and the patient are both victims, is a severe inhibitor of this process. The name that we give to this inner act is courage.

The courage to face inner fears

Silent, inner courage is something that is required both of the patient and of the psychotherapist. It is often difficult for us to appreciate fully the degree of fear that is experienced by someone when the object that creates the fear is invisible. Yet the hidden object is just as menacing—in fact, more so—than a visible object. The night before the Battle of Bosworth Field, Richard III had a dream which, he said, was worse than the full strength of Richmond's army:

> By the apostle Paul, shadows tonight
> Have struck more terror to the soul of Richard
> Than the substance of ten thousand soldiers
> Armed in truth and led by shallow Richmond.
> [Act V, Scene 3, line 217]

On one occasion, I was treating a man, a transsexual, who was trying to summon up the courage to speak to his wife about something to do with sexual relations. He said to me, "You know, I think this takes as much courage as it does to climb Mount Everest."

I think that he was quite right. With some patients, these inner objects, these tyrants that rage within the soul, are very frequently projected by the patient out of his inner world onto and into the psychotherapist. The process can be a very disconcerting experience.

I was once treating an obsessional woman when I suddenly had an image of myself as a judge at the Old Bailey with a black cap on. It was disconcerting to realize that this was exactly how the patient experienced me. In such circumstances, it takes the patient considerable courage even to get into the consulting-room where she has to face the tyrants that are now raging within her from the persona of the psychotherapist.

One of two things very frequently happens and both of them are errors as bad as each other. The psychotherapist is either moved to become persecuting towards the patient or he goes out of his way to try to reassure the patient that he is a benign figure. So in this instance, where I had this image of myself as an Old Bailey judge with a black cap on, I might have tried to reassure my patient that she had nothing to fear and that all I wanted was her welfare and to help her get better as soon as possible. However, neither of these approaches is in any way effective. On the one hand, the patient feels persecuted and paralysed, and the inner situation remains unchanged. Consequently, the patient might, for instance, leave the treatment in the belief that by leaving the psychotherapist he has resolved his problem. But, in fact, although this may give temporary relief, it is not lasting. On the other hand, the patient feels assuaged and comforted but only at a superficial level. In this case, the inner tyrant remains as active as before.

The only way forward in such circumstances is for the psychotherapist to make a drawing, as it were, of the situation as clearly as possible and show how this whole situation functions to prevent fertile creative communication between him and the patient. It is necessary to realize, of course, that this whole set-up is a defence—it has been erected for the purpose of preventing the pain and suffering that the patient feels is unbearable. So the effect, initially, when the psychotherapist interprets this, is that the patient will go through agonies and experience extreme psychic pain. The patient also feels very much more dependent on the psychotherapist, and this is frequently a source of humiliation. It takes considerable courage on the part of the psychotherapist to go through with this and be able, in a real way, to give emotional support to the patient. This situation can be extremely difficult and burdensome for the psychotherapist and nearly always requires acts of courage.

Conclusion

True pain is connected to a self-knowledge that always comes about through the agency of another. I do not mean that we do not experience painful things without it being directly pointed out to us or through contact with another, but the process by which such painful happenings occur is always in the context of a closeness to another. It is this sort of closeness that the psychotherapist is attempting to bring about, not in order to inflict pain, but in order to enable the other person to grow mentally and emotionally. Such inner emotional acts are part of the therapeutic process. The words that the psychotherapist speaks are just the vehicle carrying the emotional signals—it is summoning the courage to do it that constitutes the very heart of the therapeutic endeavour. It may seem strange that courage is a virtue required of a psychotherapist, yet I believe that, without it, we will never uncover the madness in the patient (or, for that matter, in ourselves).

CHAPTER SIX

Self-esteem
in analyst and patient

This chapter explores the following interwoven themes: the problem of unconscious resistance in the analyst, the analytic process as the third term in the analytic endeavour, and the disparity between inner identity and declared role. In order to develop these themes, I start by relating a case of mine where I was seeing a couple experiencing difficulties in their marriage.

The husband was a stockbroker and the wife looked after their two daughters at their home outside London. The husband had been in a stockbroking firm since leaving school. It was a firm that his uncle was in, and he had been taken into the company on the old boy network. He was liked by his uncle and by his two cousins, who were also partners. My patient was not an adventurous man, and I doubt whether he ever made a fortune for any of his clients, but he served them well, distributing their money across a range of investments that produced a steady capital growth together with a moderate income. There had been occasions when some of his peers murmured that Harry was not bringing in much new business, but his uncle always assuaged their grumbles by saying that Harry had a gentlemanly style of approach which was very gratifying to many of their elderly and more traditional clients, ". . . and that is where the wealth of this country still lies", he would say with an air of authority that was not to be disputed. For almost twenty years, Harry found shelter from the harsh realities of business in the contemporary world. Then his uncle died. A new chairman was appointed from outside the firm, and the organization was swept with a new broom. Each partner had to bring in a minimum amount of new business each year. Harry no longer met a comforting smile from his uncle, only an abrupt scowl from the efficient new chairman.

When husband and wife came to see me, the self-esteem of both was crumbling. Harry was only just holding his head above water and his wife, Sophia, was demoralized. Soon after the birth of their second daughter, Sophia had developed a slipped disc and had to lie flat on her back. This meant that she could not mother her new baby and so had to engage the services of a nanny. Being unable to look after her young daughter, she felt wounded at the centre of her feminine self. In this state, she attacked her husband for not being a better financial provider, and he, ever more frantic, set off to work earlier and earlier and often came back after 9 p.m. At weekends, family intimacy was impaired through the presence of the nanny, whom the wife unconsciously resented as an intruder who had robbed her of her maternal functions and whom the husband consciously resented as a further drain on their diminishing financial resources.

Role-related self-esteem

In many marriages, there still exists the traditional division of labour. We are all familiar with the traditional gender-linked roles: the husband goes to work and earns the money, the wife cooks the meals and looks after the children and tidies the house (in the 1990s we probably all know of cases where these roles are reversed). Now this division of labour may come about in two ways that are profoundly different psychologically. The first is, in fact, typified in the case of Harry and Sophia and goes something like this. The husband was the financial provider; it was a field that he knew about and his wife did not. (In the course of therapy, his wife complained that although they had been married for eleven years, he had never allowed her to visit his office.) This, anyway, was the myth, and it was here that the husband's esteem for himself was located. This was the unquestioned state of affairs when Harry and Sophia had first met. Sophia did not know about financial matters, but she knew about looking after babies and managing the home. So, underlying this division of labour was a role-relation that went something like this: the husband was the father and his wife was the daughter. This was played out in the arena of their income. For him, psychologically, she was a silly little girl who did not understand business matters. Yet, if this were so, why would he have minded letting her come to his office? Surely this could only have meant that the wife was a threat to his self-esteem.

Now the wife's self-esteem was in her ability to look after her children, cook meals, and tidy the house: this was her unquestioned attitude from the time of their first meeting and within their marriage. For her, he was a silly little boy who did not know anything about cooking, tidying the house, or looking after children. Yet when he suggested dismissing the nanny and leaving later in the morning and coming home earlier, she did not seem to want it any more than he wanted her to visit his office. The self-esteem of each partner was of a compensatory nature: they both, at the very centre of their beings and in their own ways, felt deficient and so were on the defensive, guarding against this knowledge becoming known either to the other or to themselves.

Compensatory locus in loss of self-esteem

The identity of each of them was rooted in what I would call a "compensatory locus". His self-pride was established in his capabilities as a stockbroker—but the fact that he had to keep his wife away from this is an indication that he was, in fact, lacking in the very place where his self-esteem was important. The seed, as it were, had been sown in shallow ground. The reason it was shallow was that his father (with whom his mother colluded) thought that stockbroking was the thing for Harry, and Harry had gone along with it in order to feel loved and cherished. I call it a "compensatory locus" because it is an idea about himself that he knows is false; he defends himself against his wife because he feels that she will see his deficiency and treat him sadistically—then he really will be a little boy at the mercy of the witch.

The wife's sense of self-esteem was in her ability to mother her two daughters. However, the presence of the nanny clearly demonstrated that she could not mother her daughters, and so she felt deficient. In fact, when they started coming to see me, Sophia had not had back trouble for eighteen months, but they were still employing the nanny. If the nanny were dismissed, she feared that her psychological deficiency would show up. She also kept her husband at bay and did not welcome the idea of his coming home earlier. Neither husband nor wife opened themselves to one another. Sophia feared that she would show herself to be a little girl and Harry would despise her; Harry feared to show himself as a little boy who could not manage financial affairs (which symbolized manhood for him) for he feared that if he did so Sophia would despise him. In each case, they were not grown up but felt that they should have been.

Rites of passage

One of the disjunctions between the individual and the social environment in which he is embedded occurs when his psychological development does not accompany life's rites of passage. When a man celebrates his twenty-first birthday, he believes he should be a man; when a girl marries, she believes that she should be able to mother her children and manage her house; and when a baby is born, the husband believes he should now be able to be a father. I think, though, that the rites of passage are not proclamations of an achieved state of affairs but, rather, challenges to become.

After a long training analysis, numerous clinical seminars, individual supervision, and years of attending academic seminars, I qualified as a psychoanalyst. When patients were referred to me, I believed I *should* understand their communications, and I often had the idea that my patients seemed to think so, too. I had the good fortune once to have a patient who had this idea in such an exaggerated form that the absurdity of the situation began to penetrate.

> She did not tell me she had lost her job, she expected me to know. She did not tell me that her boyfriend, Peter, had left her for another woman, she expected me to know; and she did not tell me that she had abandoned sociology and was taking up art, but expected me to know. After all, I *should* know—I was a psychoanalyst. I felt very obtuse. If I was going to get anywhere, I needed her help, and I communicated just that to her. It was a massive disappointment to her that I did not understand her unless she told me. She had longed for her mother to understand her in the early days before she could speak: she had longed for her mother intuitively to *know* when she was distressed inwardly. I think in this patient there had been some severe deprivation in the area of what Winnicott (1956) called "primary maternal preoccupation", and she believed that the analyst would be what she had always wanted so much. Only when this fantasy began to be disrupted did it become possible for the desperately disappointed baby to appear in the consulting-room. Only when I gave up my identity as someone who should understand my patients did the treatment begin to make some progress.

Action images

As analysts or psychotherapists, we do cling, or at least I cling, to "action images". By this, I mean those things that I should do and that have representations in my mind; they can be either collective or personal. What follows are some examples of collective action images.

Collective action images

While in training, I had received the traditional wisdom that one should wait at the beginning of a session until the patient spoke, and then interpret. One patient was outraged at this division of labour. At first I was stubborn and interpreted her refusal to conform as resistant and perverse (and no doubt a few other pejorative epithets). She became more and more frantic. Then I began to wonder whether it was really essential to the process that the patient start first. I decided it wasn't, and so began to start sessions, from time to time, by voicing a thought. I then realized that I quite often had a thought I wanted to voice. It then became clear what my patient's complaints had been about. Why had I held back on my thoughts when she had nothing to say and I did?

An aspect of my identity had found its locus in the dictum that the analyst must wait for the patient to start, and yet the analytic process is located in the communication flow that occurs between analyst and patient. It is there that my identity needs to be rooted, although it is more unsettling than being on the *terra firma* of a bit of dogma.

* * *

I was brought up to believe that it is important to interpret the negative transference. I once treated a mentally handicapped girl at the Tavistock who came once a week on a Thursday at 11 a.m. She was accepted into a new training centre where she was expected to arrive at 9.30 a.m., so she asked me for an early morning appointment. I told her that I was not able to do this. She then got her father to ring me to try to persuade me to change the time, her grandmother wrote to me, and her social worker rang, all pleading with me to change her session to an early morning time. But I was unable to oblige. The following Thursday, as I arrived at the Tavistock at about 10.45 a.m., the receptionist told me that my patient had arrived an hour earlier and had been racing up and down the corridors, clearly in a state of considerable agitation. When my patient came into my consulting-room, she was speaking rapidly, was unable to

sit in her chair, but could not say what was wrong. I conjec-
tured that she thought I would be furious with her for having
got these different people to ring and write to me, and also
that she was used to being indulged and was very angry that I
had not complied with her wishes. I also guessed that she
would not be conscious of her own anger. So I said to her, "I
think you feel that I am very angry with you". She went ber-
serk. With that patient, I had to abandon interpreting the negative transference in that mode—she had been so dogmatically
convinced that I was angry, she heard my interpretation as a
confirmation of her fears.

* * *

One day, a patient I was seeing four days a week refused to
leave at the end of the session. I got hot under the collar about
it and finally left the consulting-room; she left a few minutes
later. In the end, that is what I always did with her, as it was
usually only a minor inconvenience. Later on, though, I
wanted to arrange a seminar straight after her session on a
Tuesday. Consequently, I asked her if on Tuesdays she would
mind leaving directly at the end of the session. She agreed
without a murmur. That patient could not bear to experience
rigidity in me, and it was only when I had given up that rigidity and also some other rigid bits of behaviour that it was
possible to see and interpret her own very severe rigidity.
When I gave up my rigidity, she was no longer able to use me
as an object through which to deny her own rigidity, and a
benign outcome ensued.

* * *

These three action-images are all collective: letting the patient
start the session, interpreting the negative transference, and
patients leaving at the end of a fifty-minute session are all standard procedures in the therapeutic endeavour. Usually they are of
benefit to analyst and patient, but, if I cling to one of them feeling
that my self-esteem as an analyst is under threat unless I maintain
my stance at all costs, then I am being like the stockbroker who
could not let his wife visit his office.

The need for free flow between analyst and patient

All these examples are aspects of identity, based in a compensatory locus. There is trouble when an analyst's self-esteem is based on rules, procedures, and self-images that have become rigidified into "things in themselves". The more his identity is fashioned thus, the greater will be the number of patients who will remain inaccessible to him. I think it also leads to blocks occurring in a treatment. There is then a demand on the analyst for a sense of self-esteem based on a free flow between himself and the patient. Wherein lies the self-esteem for both analyst and patient? This seems to be a very important question.

The emotional reservoir

There are three entities in an analysis: the analyst, the patient, and the process. Of these three, the most important is the process. If the process is working smoothly, it draws water from the well with which to water the crops. The water is the emotional reservoir that exists in all of us, and the crops are life's contingencies, the management of which requires a certain emotional strength. A child needs to draw on this reservoir when a sibling is born and when he first goes to school. When a couple get married they need to draw on it when they have their first child, when their children grow up and leave the home, and when parents die. Finally, we all need it as we approach our own deaths. What I mean by the process is that system of action whereby a life contingency calls forth a new quantum of emotion from the emotional reservoir.

Just now, I used the phrase, "If the process is working smoothly", but I think it rarely works that way. My view may be "pathology-biased" due to my own professional experience, but I suspect that "smoothly", at least in our culture, is a pious wish and not the reality. The business of tapping the emotional reservoir for each life contingency is, I suspect, always fraught with conflict and difficulty. In such a struggle, either the individual manages to tap the reservoir or he does not. When he does not, he remains what we would call "emotionally immature" in some area of his personality and probably remains that way for the rest of his life. His life habits and attitudes adapt, and the attitudes of those in his social circle adapt. Although people are conscious of a physical deformity, they are rarely conscious of an emotional one—they adapt to it, but they do so unconsciously. Once people have adapted, they begin to feel at home with the situation and feel threatened if the person in question changes.

Sometimes an emotional cripple gets better "spontaneously" or manages to heal himself, though this is rare. Caryll Houselander (1952), in her book, *Guilt*, says that she cured herself of what she termed "ego-neurosis". I once met a man who had cured himself in a similar way. He had been an alcoholic, a drug addict, and a recidivist prisoner. He had, however, recovered and managed to lead a good family and professional life. I asked him one day to tell me some of the milestones that had led to his recovery, and he picked out several incidents which he believed had been crucial. I will mention one that was remarkable. While he was in prison, he became friendly with Fuchs, the traitor. One day he was in the library discussing his alcohol problem with Fuchs and described to him how he would make a determined act of will not to drink any more and how, when he was walking down a street and saw a pub looming up on his side of the street, he would cross over and go up the street on the other side. Fuchs shook his head and said to him, "When the will and imagination come into open conflict, the imagination always wins". This made a deep impression on him. Fuchs had located his problem in his fantasy life and from that time his psychic energies became concentrated in that area.

But we do not often meet such cases like this one or of Caryll Houselander herself. There is another category: those who are aware that something is amiss and seek the assistance of a psychotherapist.

Destruction of self-esteem in analyst and patient

My experience as an analyst is that a patient comes for treatment because he is semi-aware that there is a powerful force in him, stifling any hints of emotional striving towards growth. He comes to the analyst very largely to enlist his aid in combating this fifth columnist within. Now, the problem I want to address is this: what happens when the very thing sabotaging the psychic life of the patient also afflicts the analyst, albeit unbeknown to him? The following predicament, though fictional, will serve to illustrate.

THE DESTRUCTIVE PATIENT

A patient presented whose central difficulty stems from a "failure of engagement" between her and her mother. At depth, this was her principal difficulty. She had dealt with this situation in childhood by generating a variety of psychosomatic conditions, such as asthma and bronchitis. Through this and various other kinds of behaviour, she had managed to attract most of her mother's attention, at the expense of her siblings. However, it was only a compensatory palliative and did not satisfy. In school, she had usually managed to monopolize the teacher's attention, and for this reason she was disliked by the other children. She married soon after leaving school. She was extremely jealous of her husband's attentions, to the extent that she could not even bear him to read a newspaper. After having a baby, she went into a massive depression because the centre of attention had shifted from her to another.

RESENTMENT OF THE ANALYST

The analyst who was seeing this patient was soon struck by her desire for his special favour. After he had been seeing her for four months, he realized that, on three days a week, he had arranged to see her at 7.15 p.m. when he had not wanted to have any patients after 7 p.m. The patient used to speak in a soft but persuasive way, and, although the analyst was not aware of it, he was resentful of it. The reason he resented it was that he had a younger sister who used to whinge and whine and lure his mother's attention away from him, and he hated her. When he went into analysis, his resentment prickled his analyst who interpreted his envy and destructiveness. But the area of his real need was not reached, and so, with this patient, years later, he could only point out her destructiveness. The analyst never connected his resentment of his patient with his resentment of his younger sister: they did not look alike, their tones of voice were different, and the patient was more sophisticated and subtle than his sister had been. So he remained unaware of his hostility towards her. This was the predicament and, to all intents and purposes, it looked as though the therapy was stuck. What are the possibilities in situations such as this?

Resolving the impasse

There are two rather common outcomes to situations such as this. One is that either the analyst or the patient terminates the treatment. This occurs quite frequently and is a reasonably healthy solution—after all, there is not much point in carrying on with something that is sterile. The other outcome is that a malingering treatment situation develops which goes on and on, with the patient getting no better and the analyst deriving no satisfaction. The situation is bad for both analyst and patient and leads to the diminution of self-esteem in both. Is there any way out of this impasse?

There is another outcome and that is when either analyst or patient becomes conscious of the block. It is my observation that, in such cases, consciousness, if it occurs at all, will emerge in both partners. Either the analyst will have an insight and communicate it to the patient and the latter is ripe for receiving it, or the patient will clamour at the analyst until it dawns on him. It is a fact that if it does not dawn on the analyst, then it usually does not quite come into consciousness for the patient. I think the reason is as follows. A truth can only come to consciousness when it can be borne by each party. If a certain truth is too unbearable to the analyst, then the patient will unconsciously sense it and be unable to articulate it clearly. I think this arises because the patient does not want to hurt the analyst. It may sound strange when we know how patients getting angry with their analysts is part of our stock-in-trade, yet I believe it to be the case. This is especially so when the analyst believes he can bear the truth when he in fact cannot. As a result, the patient feels it would be a terrible blow to the analyst's self-esteem to say what he feels, it is unnerving and frightening, and so the truth remains on the brink of conscious-ness but never attains the full light of awareness. I think that human beings avoid the conjunction of knowing and hurting one of their fellows.

The process of rebuilding self-esteem

When a new truth does come to birth and awareness of it emerges in both parties, the therapy moves forward and both analyst and patient change significantly. In the case I have been describing, the patient found she no longer needed to whinge and ask for special favours to the same extent, and the analyst found he was less resentful of her and perhaps aware of a deficiency in his own analysis. Finally, he became tolerant towards his sister; his pa-tient's evident improvement enhanced his self-esteem as an analyst. The experience of integration had brought with it satisfac-tion of a deep kind. The patient experienced considerable growth in self-esteem in the knowledge that she had been able to contrib-ute to the process and not just receive the analyst's interpretations as a humble subject receives Maundy money from the Sovereign in Holy Week.

Conclusion

What, then, is this process? It is the flow from the emotional reser-voir discussed earlier. The emotional strength that we gain by tapping into that reservoir occurs in the presence of a fertilizing contact between mother and child, father and child, husband and wife, analyst and patient. There is no doubt that analyst and patient start off the endeavour with each having unconscious resistance to further emotional development. However, it is trust in the process working in each and between them which builds up their self-esteem. For both of them, self-esteem grows out of the knowledge that they have contributed to this process.

I want to go back to the married couple with whom I started. Contrary to Harry's expectations, Sophia did not despise him when she realized that he was deficient at his job. Instead, she began to make helpful suggestions that made him feel supported. When she began to have some confidence that he did not despise her for needing help in mothering, she was able to give notice to the nanny. Their acknowledgement of their deficiencies allowed them to pool their positive assets into a deposit for joint development.

There is no doubt that analyst and patient start off the endeavour each having unconscious resistances to further emotional development. However, there is a process, the third term, working in each and between them. It is trust in this process that builds up self-esteem, both in the analyst and in the patient.

CHAPTER SEVEN

Transference

T his chapter is based on three papers, respectively entitled: "The Erotic Transference and Boundaries", "The Negative Transference", and "Countertransference". They are here combined under the one general heading.

Interpreting the transference is the single factor that most clearly differentiates psychotherapy that has been derived from psychoanalysis from other therapies. One would expect, therefore, that this would be clearly understood by all psychotherapists and also that it would be at the very centre of any psychotherapist's education, yet I think that it usually falls into second place. It is also not well understood—at least, it is not understood emotionally. At the most simple level, the transference constitutes those feelings that the patient has towards his psychotherapist. It is difficult to talk about the feelings that one person has towards you. Nearly all conversations that we conduct in our social lives avoid this particular area of expression. To get at why it is awkward and difficult is not quite so easy, but some understanding of it may come as we proceed. Let it remain as a fact that it is something that is exceedingly difficult for us emotionally, and for this reason the psychotherapist as well as the patient will try to avoid it.

The erotic transference

It was the interpretation of the erotic transference that changed Freud from being a hypnotist and using a therapy associated with hypnosis to being a psychoanalyst. Freud came to realize that the hypnotic trance came about through the presence of an erotic factor. I will quote Freud (1925d [1924]) on how this realization was borne in on him.

> One day I had an experience which showed me in the crudest light what I had long suspected. It related to one of my most acquiescent patients, with whom hypnotism had enabled me to bring about the most marvellous results, and whom I was engaged in relieving of her suffering by tracing back her attacks of pain to their origins. As she woke on one occasion, she threw her arms around my neck. The unexpected entrance of a servant relieved us from a painful discussion, but from that time onwards there was a tacit understanding between us that the hypnotic treatment should be discontinued. I was modest enough not to attribute the event to my own irresistible personal attraction, and I felt that I had now grasped the nature of the mysterious element that was at work behind hypnotism. In order to exclude it, or at all events to isolate it, it was necessary to abandon hypnotism. [p. 27]

It was the interpretation of this erotic element that then allowed Freud to trace back first to the flowerings of sexuality in adolescence, and then back further to the time when, as a child, the patient first fell in love—that is, with his own parents.

The first and most straightforward level of erotic transference, which frequently occurs, is when the female patient feels sexually aroused by the male psychotherapist and consequently desires the psychotherapist to make love to her. It is exactly the same the other way round, when a male patient finds that he wants to make love to his female psychotherapist. Very often this form of transference occurs early on in the treatment situation—usually within the first twenty sessions. The psychotherapist has a task, which is to help his patient grow emotionally and to resolve the deep problems that confront him in his life, but the sexual feelings that have arisen are an obstacle. The psychotherapist has just one course open to him, that is, to put into words to his patient the feelings that have arisen. If this is done clearly and honestly, the patient experiences relief, because he feels that the psychotherapist is not too troubled by this potential difficulty and is concerned to get on with the task. There is an unhealthy side of the patient, the resistant side, which may get angry and may also find it rather.a blow to his sense of sexual self-esteem, but the healthy side will be relieved and glad that matters have been cleared up so that the task of treatment can be addressed.

It looks as though it should be quite an easy and a straightforward matter, yet time and again erotic and sexual feelings arise in the patient towards the psychotherapist that the psychotherapist fails to interpret. A frequent outcome of this situation is that the patient gives up the treatment.

> I once interviewed a girl who had first gone to another psychotherapist. It was not clear why she had left the other psychotherapist until she mentioned with some embarrassment that he was just about her age. Then it emerged that she had felt sexual attraction for him, felt awkward about it, and left. The psychotherapist had said nothing about it.

There are many permutations of this basic phenomenon, and there is a widely variegated array of this particular type of transference.

The sexual and the erotic

The word "sexual" is used here as it would be used by the man in the street—that is, feelings that are aroused in the genital area in the presence of a stimulating object, most obviously by a member of the opposite sex, but sometimes by someone of the same sex. "The erotic" I will define as those feelings that come from sublimated sexual energy. So, a mother's love for her baby is erotic—it always has a sensual element. This sensual element creates an attachment between two people—mother and baby, child and its father, brothers and sisters, and so on. Bodily parts can also exert erotic attraction—hair colour, tone of voice, style of movement, colour of eyes, gestures, and so on. Hatred also has an erotic quality in it, especially when there is disgust and contempt. It is by no means neutral. It has been brought out quite well in literature that there can be an attraction, sometimes a fatal attraction, for what is repulsive and disgusting. The most important qualities of the erotic are its depth, its intensity, and its hiddenness.

Defence mechanisms against erotic attraction

This last quality of the erotic, its hiddenness, is a product of shame. The patient feels ashamed and overwhelmed to find himself enveloped in powerful erotic feelings towards his psychotherapist and develops a defence mechanism to fight those feelings. Frequently, at the beginning of treatment, a patient starts a sexual affair in order to protect himself from the full strength of the feelings that come up in the transference—the strength of those feelings can be frightening. Sometimes a patient protects himself against these powerful feelings for the whole duration of a long analysis. To his friends, it can be a matter of some astonishment that such an apparently unsuitable liaison continues year after year: the key to it is that the liaison is being used to protect the patient against the strength of his feelings. There are many variations of it: some patients will have a long period of intensified promiscuity; others will suddenly start, for no apparent reason, a homosexual affair; another may announce at the very beginning of the treatment that he is going to get married. The other version of this is the patient who suddenly terminates an affair at the beginning of treatment. This is because he believes that the psychotherapist is intensely jealous of the affair. In nearly all these cases, the patient is very finely attuned to the psychotherapist, and such actions as starting a sexual liaison, finishing it, or altering its emotional content are very frequently generated by changes in the psychotherapist's emotional attitude. I have seen this again and again; I have also noted from supervising people that psychotherapists (including myself) are often not aware that all these activities are expressive products of the erotic transference.

I want to labour this point because, although it is the foundation stone of psychotherapy, I believe that our grasp of it is woefully inadequate. I expect this is because it is too unsettling for a psychotherapist to realize that his own "innocent" actions, interventions, or interpretations can have an effect that penetrates a person's emotional sexual life to an extent that can be thoroughly alarming.

Therapy and the patient's sex life

The following is an example, perhaps a rather crude one, that illustrates the way in which the emotional interaction in the consulting-room is intimately linked to the sexual occurrences in the patient's life.

When I was in London, a colleague of mine who was going on sabbatical for a year asked me if he could give my name to his patients so that they could contact me if they were in any crisis. I agreed, so he gave me a list of the patients in question. He had been away for about six months when one of his patients, Sophia, rang and asked if she could come and see me. During the consultation, it transpired that over the previous eighteen months she had had two affairs, both of which had broken up because of the men's impotence. Now she had started another affair with a new man, called Michael. It had been going well for about six weeks until he had started to lose his erection just at the point when he was about to make love to her. This appalled her and also panicked her, because it had been the same with the previous two men and she began to feel that there must be something wrong with her.

I was in something of a quandary as to what to do: I did not want to take her into long-term treatment as my colleague was due back in six months, yet it was clear that I could not just leave her to her fate. I decided that this was a fairly isolated behavioural sexual symptom, so I offered her a brief contract of twenty sessions with the whole focus on her sexual predicament. She was an extremely sexual woman with a strong, vibrant personality. Two or three sessions passed in which she told me about the deteriorating situation with Michael, how every time he tried to make love to her his penis detumesced.

She also told me a bit about her background. I felt rather hope-less and knew I was not getting very far. Then in the fourth session something began to clarify in my mind, a pattern be-gan to emerge. Just as I was about to put it into words in the form of an interpretation, I found to my dismay that I lost it. I felt mildly irritated. Later in the session something again be-gan to clarify and to formulate itself in my mind. I was about to speak when once more she said something and I completely lost the thread of what I was going to say. And in the next session, the same thing happened after about ten minutes, again after about half an hour, and again shortly before the end of the session. By the end of the session and when she had left, I became convinced that this phenomenon was the centre of what I had to address. I also made the connection between the thing happening in my mind and what was happening to the penis of the man trying to make love to her. When she came for the next session, I put all my energies into the task that confronted me. I moved my chair a bit further from her at the beginning of the session and let her speak. Something again began to formulate itself in my mind, and as it became clearer I stopped her talking, told her that I had something to say, and said it—I did not lose it. It went in, and I could tell that she was annoyed. But what I had said continued to be developed during the rest of the session. At the next session, she wore a radiant smile. She told me that on the Thursday evening (Thursday was the day of the week when I saw her), Michael had come around to see her, and they had gone to bed together. He had maintained his erection and made love to her in a satisfactory way. She then said she did not know why, but she had some idea that it was connected with the session on the same day.

As I said at the beginning, this is a rather crude example of the link between the emotional processes going on in the therapeutic session and the sexual happenings outside the session. She had never previously been able to sustain a relationship with a man for more than a few months. When my colleague came back from his sabbatical, she returned to him, and, at the same time, her relationship with Michael broke up. Why had I been so fainthearted? Why had I not kept her in treatment? Was a six-month affair all I could manage, else why hand her back to a colleague?

Treatment of erotic transference

The crucial factor that enables the patient to let go of the erotic transference is through the psychotherapist holding the treatment boundaries as firmly as possible. In the presence of a powerful erotic transference, which is also always manifest in a terrific idealization, the very smallest actions are interpreted by the patient as signs of the psychotherapist's state of being "in love". In that hypersensitized state, the smallest actions are interpreted in terms of attachment or of rejection.

- A male patient was seeing a female psychotherapist in London. He spoke of a holiday he was taking in Wales and how the bedroom was big enough for two. He went on and on about this until the psychotherapist realized that the patient believed that she was going with him. He had become convinced of this because he had noticed a book on Wales on her bookshelf.

- In another case, a patient believed that the psychotherapist was his girlfriend because, although he knew she lived with a man, she never mentioned him. He therefore assumed that meant she was no longer involved with the other man and was now really in love with him. When this was interpreted and clarified, the patient embarked on a sexual relationship with a woman which was more satisfactory than previous attempts.

The perception that the psychotherapist is there to offer treatment and not to be a sexual or erotic partner needs to be interpreted again and again, each time at a deeper level. As it is interpreted and worked through, the patient's inner structure becomes more robust and his own sexual and emotional life becomes noticeably strengthened.

The psychotherapist needs to recognize that the erotic transference is a phenomenon that occurs in one of its many different forms with every patient who enters the consulting-room. It is then the psychotherapist's task to grasp what the erotic transference is and how it is functioning between the patient and himself, and to interpret it when he gets some understanding of it.

The negative transference

There is so much misconception about the negative transference that I want to start off by explaining what it is not. When the psychotherapist instigates or, I might say, manipulates the patient into anger, this is not negative transference. Neither is it negative transference when the psychotherapist misunderstands the patient and evokes a hostile reaction. I need to emphasize this, because very often I have heard these processes wrongly referred to as the negative transference. This is a mistake that can lead to people complaining when the negative transference is used in a way that is thought to be harmful to the patient, whereas in fact what has happened is one of the processes that I have just described. Misconceptions about the nature of the negative transference can result in the psychotherapist remaining uninstructed in the delicate task of detecting it, although in any course of treatment it is always present at various points.

The negative transference expressed openly

The psychotherapist is always engaged in a process that is painful for the patient. The patient views this inflictor of pain with suspicion, hostility, anger, contempt, or rage. Alternatively, the patient feels ashamed or humiliated in the presence of the psychotherapist. However, the psychotherapist is engaged in an activity that cannot but evoke one or more of these negative emotions—it is inherent in his relationship with his patient.

Sometimes the negative transference is clear. On one occasion it was obvious, in the very first session, that the patient oozed hatred towards me:

It was so vehement that when she walked past me at the end of the session, her head twitched. In the eleventh session, the dam burst, and she exploded with a torrent of fury at me. She said that she thought I was a monster, that she wondered why Hitler had not used psychoanalysts as his SS men as they would be far more effective torturers than the SS men. She also said she would write to General Pinochet and give him the name of an exceedingly effective torturer whom she felt he could use. She went on like this for about half an hour—in fact, until the end of the session.

Now, I think this was quite a healthy response at the beginning of treatment: she was a very passionate woman and had not managed to get direction into her life. In the initial interview, she had blamed most of her misfortunes on those around her. She was now acting in a similar way—but the person she was blaming for her present misfortune was me. The healthy side of it was that she was showing me in a very direct way the sort of impulses that came out of her and which led people to treat her badly. It was also possible to see the way she became submissive, out of guilt, when she realized she had harboured such hostile feelings towards people of significance in her life. Now, it is possible that I had provoked this patient somewhat, and in fact, in the session prior to the one I have described, I think I had. In that session, I said to her that I thought she felt I was a monster. Although I think what I said was true, I also said it because the atmosphere of hostility in the consulting-room was so intense that I wanted some relief from it, even to the extent of provoking a reaction. However, I think that the intensity of her outburst was out of proportion to the provocation. I would conjecture, therefore, that she was superimposing upon me the imago of an inner figure which was extremely torturing to her.

For about eighteen months, this patient experienced me as a very powerful and dangerous figure. She was exceedingly wary of me, always very suspicious, and constantly believing that I would do the dirty on her in one way or another. Then a change took place—I was now being cast in the role of her elder sister and also her mother, both of whom had treated her in a way that caused her enormous disappointment. More deeply, I was also the receptacle of an inner figure that had truly tortured her and messed up her life pretty thoroughly. She had submitted herself to a very prolonged sexual affair with a man who made all sorts of promises which he did not keep. When she finally left him, she shacked up with a series of men who also treated her badly. She was a woman of very exceptional talent and capability, but she had never achieved anything approaching her potential. This was because she was tortured and pushed down by a repressive inner figure. I had become in the transference the receptacle of this inner figure. There were occasions when I became quite frightened of her, and I used to ensure that there were no potentially dangerous implements in the room with which she might attack me. I do not at this juncture want to go into those aspects of her impulses that had contributed to the manufacture of this inner figure.

I mention this example because the negative transference was so very evident—this patient did not have much difficulty in giving expression to it. In many ways, I think a psychotherapist is lucky to have a patient who gives expression to the negative transference so openly. In my experience, the majority of patients try in all sorts of subtle ways to mask the negative transference. However, if the psychotherapist firmly makes contact with the healthy aspects of the personality and manages to put a firm boundary around envy, omnipotence, and narcissism, the patient will ultimately experience relief. But the immediate reaction is one of hostility: the patient will experience the psychotherapist as uncaring, hateful, only concerned with himself, and so on. This is the unhealthy infantile side battering against the alliance between the healthy side of the patient and the psychotherapist who keeps in contact with it. If the psychotherapist is not doing this, then he will not get a negative transference. It is only when the psychotherapist firmly addresses the destructive and unhealthy aspects of the personality that he experiences the negative transference.

Recognizing and receiving the negative transference

One of the areas in which the psychotherapist needs finely tuned sensitivity is in distinguishing between the negative transference and straightforward justifiable negativity. So let us try to formulate what is going on. It is the healthy part of the personality that wants the psychotherapist to make contact with it and help it become the dominant force in the person's life. Then there is an unhealthy part that does not want the psychotherapist's healthy intervention but wants to keep the patient in a state of sickness or a state of retarded emotional development. From the first side, the healthy side, comes healthy self-assertion. From the other side comes the negative transference.

One of the most important things is that when the negative transference emerges, the psychotherapist is prepared to receive it and does not repudiate it. This is such an important matter that I want to dwell on it a little further. For most of us, it goes against the grain to be accused of insensitivity, self-centredness, narrow-mindedness, or any other such designation. When a patient tells the psychotherapist in the initial interview that her mother never took an interest in what she herself really wanted, you can be sure that when the psychotherapist begins to tackle this patient's destructive side and to put some ballast behind the healthy side, the patient will then feel the psychotherapist to be taking no interest in her. She will experience the psychotherapist in the same way as she experienced her mother. When the patient starts to feel this, one of two things may happen. If the psychotherapist is lucky, the patient will begin to say that she feels that the psychotherapist has no interest in her. But it is more likely that the patient will begin to withdraw, perhaps cancel a session, perhaps begin to come late or show no interest. It is the psychotherapist's task to realize that the patient is beginning to experience him as not having any interest in her, and he then needs to make an interpretation to that effect. If he does this with the right emphasis at the right moment, the patient will usually acknowledge it and perhaps elaborate the matter a little further. The patient has transplanted this noxious inner introject into the psychotherapist, and, because it is not lodged within his psychic structure any more, the healing forces are able to get to work within him. In other words, if the psychotherapist is first able to recognize the negative transference and then interprets it—and all the while is able to receive it and not repudiate it—this enables the patient to mobilize the healing processes within himself.

The reason I emphasize this is that I know from personal experience, and also from supervising people and from hearing clinical presentations, that it is something exceedingly difficult for a psychotherapist to perceive. There is no doubt that it is indeed exceedingly difficult to be designated and perceived in an unpleasant light. What the psychotherapist must do is get some sense of the negative image that is being attributed to him and then speak from it. If, as a psychotherapist, you can get the picture of yourself as a rigid authoritarian figure, or a dull idiot, or an enfeebled figure who needs to be looked after, and realize that the patient is casting you in this role rather as a theatre manager might cast you in such a role for a play, then you can with greater ease interpret the patient's feelings.

> For instance, a patient of mine cast me in the role of a depressed, unhappy figure who needed him as a prop to make my life bearable. When he missed a session and was exaggeratedly anxious, I told him that he felt I would be very depressed and hardly able to manage for the rest of the day without the consolation and comfort that each session with him brought me. I had access to his feelings. Those *were* his feelings. It was also possible to interpret at another point his extreme anger at having to support this doddering old analyst in this way. After all, he was paying me to treat him, making a long journey several times a week to visit me, and he felt bitterly resentful that, rather than me help him, he was having to prop me up. You must note that I did not say this was the case—I just interpreted his feelings about it. I could not have had such accurate access to his feelings had I not had such a clear image of the sad doddering figure that he supposed me to be. We often preach to the patient what his feelings *should* be rather than interpret what they *are*.

One might ask whether there is any value in putting such absurd feelings into words. The understanding of the patient's real feelings is the central therapeutic factor. It is through them that the psychotherapist enters into the patient's inner world. So it was with my patient—he was spending all his psychic energies in propping up a doddering inner figure. I was able to enter into an understanding of this, to participate in his inner drama and have some understanding of what it was like to be him. This kind of very real understanding is the healing factor. I understood in a living way what he was carrying around.

What I am saying, therefore, is that the psychotherapist needs to receive the negative imago, but does he do so *ad infinitum*? My experience is that the patient will give some sign when he is ready to move on. It is then possible to show the patient the way he clings, despite much evidence to the contrary, to this image. I did this with the man in question. He was then ready to cast off this inner illusory figure and in fact did so. From that time on, he became markedly more robust in his professional and social life. So it is a mistake to indulge the negative transference for too long—a time will come when the patient is ready to move on.

However, there is one type of patient with whom it is definitely a mistake clinically to receive the negative imago. This is the patient who bears no inner responsibility for anything, blaming his misfortunes entirely on others. If the psychotherapist offers himself in the way I have been suggesting, the patient will, with delight, take the opportunity to continue escaping responsibility for his life. In such a case, the psychotherapist needs to show the patient how he blames father, mother, brothers, sisters, and now the psychotherapist for all his misfortunes. Only then will the patient begin to take responsibility for his own inner and outer actions and begin to have the space for an inner world where feeling and thinking can go on.

The importance of a correct interpretation

I think it is very difficult for any of us if someone calls us greedy or envious or insensitive or omnipotent: coming to terms with these aspects of ourselves is, in fact, an ongoing struggle. The capacity to take the negative transference is co-extensive with that struggle to come to terms with the shadow side of ourselves, as Jung (1975, p. 20) put it. Yet I believe that the interpretation of the negative transference is essential. It is possible to end a treatment without any interpretation of the negative transference or even allowing it to surface at all. It can look as though the treatment has worked very well: the patient may leave with the appearance of being in good health with manifest signs of neurosis gone. However, I believe such a cure is of short duration. John Klauber, author of *Difficulties in the Analytic Encounter* (1981a), used to say that the analyst needs to have his mind focused on the period of time that stretches from the day the patient leaves the consulting-room for the last time to the day of his death. It is that long-term perspective that I am talking of. I do not believe that a lasting foundation for the rest of the patient's life will be achieved unless the negative transference is allowed to surface and is then interpreted in the way I have tried to describe. It is a difficult task—but, if we want long-term effects, then we must attempt it.

The countertransference

Freud referred to the countertransference, but only rarely, and Jung did not make much use of the term. The first analyst to devote a paper to the subject was Winnicott, in 1947, in his paper "Hate in the Countertransference". This was followed three years later by Paula Heimann's paper "On Countertransference". The latter paper is a classic and has remained a seminal paper within psychoanalysis. It would be difficult today to imagine doing psychotherapy without an awareness of countertransference. Countertransference, like transference, is a phenomenon, it is not a theory. When we start to conceptualize how it comes about we enter the field of hypothesis and theory. It is necessary to distinguish between transference and countertransference as accurately as possible.

Defining countertransference

I have often heard psychotherapists make statements such as these: "I reflected on my countertransference . . .", "In the counter-transference I felt . . .", and "My countertransference told me . . .". All these statements refer to a situation in which the psychotherapist quite easily summons up his observing ego. This is one use of the term, but I believe that it is confusing to use it in this way. I think here the psychotherapist is aware of his feelings in relation to the patient and makes interpretations accordingly. If we use countertransference in this way, then all the feelings that the psychotherapist has would have to be included under the heading of countertransference. This so generalizes the term as to render it meaningless.

When we use the term "countertransference" as it is applied to a psychotherapist, we mean that some aspect of the person's perceptual or mental apparatus is not functioning—I would prefer the term to define those occasions when the psychotherapist's functioning ego is not able to summon an interpretation. This phenomenological state can be divided into two types. The first type is where the psychotherapist is aware of the feeling but is unable to understand it and therefore not able to make an interpretation. I will call this a Mode One countertransference. The second type is where the psychotherapist is not aware of a feeling and instead enacts something. I will call this a Mode Two counter-transference.

Mode One countertransference

In this mode, the psychotherapist is aware of a feeling, but there is no understanding of it. The following case will serve as an illustration.

I was once treating a woman who had a job as a personnel manager's assistant. She came to me because in the past she kept losing her job, and now that she had landed the best job she'd ever had she wanted to ensure that she didn't lose it. She came on time for each session and paid dutifully at the end of each month. She listened carefully to interpretations and said that the therapy was a great help to her and that relations with her husband and mother seemed to improve. I had every reason to feel satisfied with the way the treatment was going. She could be described as a model patient. If the psychotherapist treating that patient had any complaints, then you might be justified in calling him a malcontent. Well, this psychotherapist who *was* treating her had a very big complaint: he was bored stiff with her. He could hardly drag himself into the consulting-room to see her. He wished it was Mr. P or Miss L that he was seeing for the next session, but here he was once again landed with Miss X. And would she ever miss a session? No such luck.

This was a Mode One countertransference: I was aware that the boredom was something that I was registering from the patient, but what I lacked was any understanding of it. My feelings were intact but my capacity to understand was completely deficient, although my capacity to understand was operating perfectly well with other patients and even with this particular patient in other aspects of her communications. So the malfunctioning was quite localized; it was only in relation to this particular patient and to one aspect of our relationship. Now it would be a fair point to make that the intense boredom that existed in relation to this patient was in me and not in her, so would it not be fair to say that it had nothing to do with her? I do not think that the evidence is in favour of this supposition. I was not bored with the patient I saw before her or the patient I saw after her and, as far as I remember, I was not bored with any of my other patients whom I was seeing at that time, and I did not see her late in the day.

It could be argued that another psychotherapist might not have been bored with this patient, or that I am particularly prone to being bored. Both these statements might well be true—the second statement I would be more able to substantiate than the first. Let us say, for a moment, that I am prone to boredom more than the average for a middle-aged, middle-class man. If this were the case, then I might need to look into it, take account of it when I am making judgements about people, and so on. However, the fact that this boredom only grinds into action when Miss X enters the consulting-room and at no other time is a fact, and a fact I need to take account of. I believe that it is necessary to attribute to Miss X some stimulus that sets the boredom going in me. That I do not understand the boredom means that my intelligence is not functioning in relation to this phenomenon.

There was one piece of information that led me to think that perhaps I was not the only person in this patient's world who suffered boredom in her presence.

I mentioned that she came because she kept losing her jobs, one after another. As she began to explain these occurrences to me, a certain pattern began to emerge. The boss would call her in and say that no one had any complaint with her work—in fact, her work was above average. But unfortunately the firm had to cut back because its profits no longer justified her position continuing. He would, of course, give her a very good reference. Quite why the boss, when he had to cut back, chose Miss X as the victim was never clear. I noticed a similarity between the attitude of her boss and my own inner attitude. If I had to cut back on my work because my health could no longer stand such long hours, I could imagine summoning Miss X and saying that, although she was an excellent patient and had made very good use of her therapy, my doctor had told me I must reduce my hours of work. Consequently, I would have to terminate her therapy, but I could, if she wanted, refer her to a very good psychotherapist. And it was not just one boss who had given her the sack, but several. Was it just possible, I said to myself, that these other people were also bored out of their minds by Miss X? It was at least a good working hypothesis. What is more, if this were the case, then boredom was the most important thing happening in this therapy. If I could resolve it, understand it, then the patient might be freed of the very thing she had come to see me about. It might even mean that all other communication and interpretations were secondary compared to this. It also occurred to me that if I did not solve this, although people might say that I was a very good psychotherapist (as was witnessed by the fact that Miss X came so regularly and reported many improvements), were I to apply for another job as a psychotherapist, I might be told how very well my work was appreciated but unfortunately my services were not required at the moment. So I must back my hypothesis and stake everything on the one unsolved clue: the fact that I found myself so terribly bored by Miss X.

I will try to unravel for you what lay behind this boredom and pass from phenomenon to a piece of personal theory: that when I have a feeling, it is *always* connected to the person in whose company I am at the time. My only evidence for this is a series of personal experiences which seems to confirm it as a fact, but the explanation of this fact requires a considerable theoretical edifice to support it. A feeling in one person is generated by another who is in close proximity. There is a lot in the psychological literature about the agency through which feelings are generated, such as through the eyes, tone of voice, quality of movement, or smell. This implies, however, that there is a discharge from one and a reception of the discharge in the other. The discharge can only occur in the presence of an object-receptor for the discharge—for one human being the only receptor is another human being. Each human being has apertures through which he discharges and also apertures through which he receives the charge. I think the apertures are also transformers. The pure charge of feeling is transformed into a perceptual medium, whether it be the medium of the eyes, voice, movement, or smell, through which it travels until meeting the aperture or receptor of the other person. This receptor transforms the perceptual medium back into pure feelings. This is, I believe, *how* it happens. It is able to happen because there is a connaturality of element. By this I mean that the crude feeling can only pass from one object to another object on condition that there is a connaturality between that feeling and the object, and also between that object and another object. This theory about the way in which one person can generate feelings in another I call the "Connaturality of Element" theory. I want now to return to Miss X.

Miss X frequently said that she thought she must be a burden to me. I believe she knew she was generating this terrible boredom in me, and she wished me to agree with her in order to alleviate her guilt. I am not sure whether psychiatrists have invented an anti-guilt pill, but, if they have, that is what she wanted from me. It would have been a palliative comment if I had said, "So you feel that you are too big a burden to me". That is, of course, the psychotherapist's way of saying, "Not at all, dear, you are not a burden at all". With the Connaturality of Element theory firmly in mind, I said, "You sense that you are doing something which you suspect makes you a burden to me". I said this in a variety of forms but the meaning was always similar. I think this made her realize that the only way out of this impasse was to stop boring me, so she did. I had closed my aperture and turned off my transformer. She herself then experienced her life as enormously boring. It then began to be possible to analyse the reasons for this. At an early stage in her life, she had retreated to live in a narcissistic cocoon. It is very boring to live cocooned with no emotional contact with any other human being. By this stage, I was not at all bored but much engaged in trying to unravel with her the reasons for this cocoon state. The Mode One countertransference was over. It was also gratifying to note that in her new job, people responded to her in a lively way, asking her to parties and so on. Such events were unheard of in her life before.

Mode Two countertransference

The type of countertransference that I have just described is a benign one. I was aware of the fact that being bored was a countertransference phenomenon, the situation of being bored continued for some time, and then finally understanding came about and the countertransference lifted. In the case of a Mode Two countertransference, however, the power of it is more virulent, and a further element of mental functioning in the psychotherapist is obliterated: it is not just the intelligence with the corresponding understanding that is affected but also the feeling itself. The psychotherapist acts but, because it is so intense, is not aware of the feeling. The next case illustrates such a countertransference.

> A female psychotherapist who was single and childless was treating a woman aged about 38. The patient had started living with a man whom the psychotherapist knew and towards whom she was antagonistic. When the patient announced that she was going to get herself pregnant, the psychotherapist told her that what she was about to do was an immature act and, as a psychotherapist, had to advise her that it was against the interests of her therapy. The psychotherapist's supervisor was alarmed by this report and suggested that she consider whether her own personal feelings had motivated such an outburst. The following week, the psychotherapist was honest enough to say that she realized that she had been intensely jealous of her patient's association with this man and was desperately envious of the girl's possible pregnancy. The psychotherapist was now in possession of two feelings—jealousy and envy—that she had not possessed when her patient announced her plan to become pregnant. I have no doubt that her envy and jealousy were generated in a similar way that the boredom was generated in me by Miss X. I want to make it clear that Miss X could not have generated this boredom without my acceptance of it. At a level below the threshold of awareness, I opened the door and allowed boredom to come in. In a similar way, the female psychotherapist invited in the jealousy and envy. She was predisposed—and the patient made the most of it.

The pressures countertransference can exert

We have all heard dreadful stories of things that analysts or psychotherapists have done. When a patient comes to see me and tells me the dreadful thing that such and such a psychotherapist did, it nearly always turns out that the patient contributed to the situation. It is, of course, the psychotherapist's job to try to avoid acting in a Mode Two manner, but it is well worth recognizing that a patient can put the psychotherapist under tremendous pressure. Countertransference can be enormously powerful, and that power is often underestimated.

> For instance, a psychotherapist interviewed a patient who came in great fury because a previous psychotherapist had suddenly shouted abuse at her. The new psychotherapist was indignant, quite sure that she would never do such a thing. She soon found, however, that this patient put her under tremendous pressure to see her more frequently than she wished—she found that even on leave she was agreeing to see her. When she was about to go away on holiday, the psychotherapist found that the patient made her feel so guilty about it that she put off telling her. Soon she found she was falling into the same trap as the first psychotherapist and was on the verge of shouting at her.

Many patients generate guilt in psychotherapists, and this can militate against therapeutic change and be just as injurious as jealousy or envy. It is one of the reasons why I am not in favour of preaching virtues at psychotherapists, because patients can so easily activate guilt through this. I would even be wary of the empathic stance so recommended by Kohut. If this has been preached at a psychotherapist, he is likely to feel guilty when he finds he is hostile towards a patient.

The Mode Two countertransference is unfortunate, but I believe it is a frequent occurrence from which none of us is immune.

> I was once treating a man into whose life there suddenly erupted a domineering woman who swept him up—within two days he was going to marry her. She had insisted that he give up his present career. To me it looked crazy: his career had been his whole adult life, and he had reached a level in his profession appropriate to his age. Now, all of a sudden, this woman steps in and sweeps him out of it. This development also meant that his treatment with me would come to an end. Although I felt strongly that I should try to dissuade him, I also felt absolutely sure that I was being set up to do just that, with the result that he would rebel against this benign tyrant

analyst. So I held my breath and did not say a word against the course of action he was intent upon. The woman came from another country, and he was going to travel with her to be married there. He told me the date of his return. I held my breath. When he returned he told me that five days before the wedding he had called it off. I had an intuition that my tactic had been right, but the inner pressure that he put on me to act differently was tremendous.

Conclusion

There are different levels of transference, starting with surface feelings that are reasonably easy to detect, to much deeper feelings and emotional configurations that can be bizarre and alarming. One might question whether it is really necessary to make transference interpretations for a therapy to be successful. If we talk with a patient about his problems, it may give him some illumination that he might find useful, but that illumination remains at the cognitive level. He may see it and understand it but be unable to apply it. Emotional change takes place only through interpretations that bear on the transference. This does not mean that other interpretations have no value, but it is in the direct feelings between the psychotherapist and the patient, and their interpretation and enactment, that emotional change is brought about.

PART TWO

PROFESSIONAL DILEMMAS

Some of the mistakes inherent in part one have been corrected here in part two. In particular, there is a greater focus upon inner activities that are destructive of healthy emotional functioning. Also, there is a developing focus on values and a conviction that the disease of *moral amorphism*, as the Russian philosopher Vladimir Solovyof (1918, p. xxviii) called it, has caught hold of the psychotherapy movement in a way that has a disastrous consequence for the emotional health of those who seek psychotherapy for their problems. To put it crudely, it is possible to think psychologically of human beings in two modes: as being acted on by their social environment and as responsive to and fashioning that environment. In psychotherapy, it is a mistake to overemphasize either side of this divide. When I was working at the Tavistock I found it necessary (or so I thought) to emphasize the former, whereas when I encountered psychotherapists in Australia I had to reverse this and emphasize the latter. By overemphasizing the former, the psychotherapist runs the risk of colluding with omnipotence; by overemphasizing the latter, he runs the risk of endorsing inner paranoia.

Some may take exception to chapter fourteen, in which I discuss the autonomy of the self. Two things need to be said about this—one is a general matter, the other particular. One of the most discouraging pieces of group symptomatology within the psychotherapy movement is psychotherapists' un-alloyed devotion to a particular clinical theorist. There are clinical groups in which it would be a sacrilege to criticize Klein; there are others that would banish anyone who impugns Winnicott, and still others whose devotion is to Fairbairn, Bion, Mahler, Freud, Jung, Lacan, or Kohut. Uncritical devotion to these figures arises through psychotherapists projecting their emotional selves into the imago of their hero. I try to describe something of this process in chapter ten, "Mimesis in Narcissistic Patients".

I am quite aware of the enormous contribution to knowledge that all these clinicians have made, but I make no apology for criticizing their views. I criticize Kohut from two general directions. One is that he did not think through his position in a radical way but only pasted his more humane attitude onto the ego psychology of Hartmann, whom he attacks so vehemently. In this, Kohut's position is shared by many others. I think only Freud, Jung, Fairbairn, and Bion radically thought through the implications of their insights. All others just pasted their positions onto a pre-existing theory, with which they do not fit. The other direction is that Kohut gives no account of inner psychic action within human beings, and so all his emphasis has been upon the fashioning environment and has neglected the reverse side of this. Thus his orientation is the emotional correlate of that of Skinner and the behaviourists and passes over what I have called elsewhere the religious model of man (Symington, 1994). My critique of Kohut is part of a more general critique of Western culture, a culture that has become barren of those core values without which we risk the depredations of political tyrants, of which this century has seen quite enough. I hope readers will see this critique within that wider context.

The chapters in part two are, then, just the first gropings towards a psychology that will be more satisfactory for the practising psychotherapist than is available at present. They are very defective, and I would ask the reader to try to grasp the spirit of what is being said rather than its expression, which I know is inadequate.

CHAPTER EIGHT

Modes of cure in psychotherapy

In the world of psychodynamic psychotherapy, there are many different schools of practice, and among these schools are competing theories and values, each with their passionate disciples. I believe that, from all of them, two theories can be distilled that concern what it is that cures a patient of his psychological illness. These two theories I will call "Cure through Understanding" and "Cure through Knowledge".

The patient who comes to the psychotherapist is in distress and it is the task of the psychotherapist to understand the patient's inner difficulties. What follows is an account of a man who came to me for treatment and my attempts at understanding him.

Understanding the patient

Stuart was in his mid-40s and, although a man of many talents, had never persevered sufficiently with any of them to have capitalized on his undoubted capabilities. He was therefore only moderately successful, with a foot in several camps. He was the kind of man who is very entertaining at parties; he also had a marriage that was crumbling. Stuart had a younger brother, Tony, who had contracted polio as a baby and had been left severely paralysed. When they were children, their mother devoted her attentions to Tony, and, to make things as easy as possible for her, Stuart had felt obliged to present himself as someone who never had any problems. As he did well at school and made many friends, all seemed well. "Stuart's always all right," was the catchword at home. He also presented himself to me as being someone with few worries.

"Janice [his wife] thought it would be a good idea if I came along", he said to me cheerily. Had his marriage not been crumbling, he certainly would not have come to see me. Stuart came because he was emotionally very dependent upon his wife, like a small boy clinging to his mother. He used to say frequently, "I don't think I need to see you, really". At the end of a session, he used to say, "Oh, well, I enjoyed that little chat". I said to him that he believed that he did not have my attention, so it was better to keep everything at the level of a "chat". In addition, I interpreted how much he hated not only the patient who came before him, but also me for the attention I gave that patient. In his mind, that patient was Tony. I conveyed my understanding of how he felt now that he was losing his wife's attention (she had started an affair with another man). As the therapy progressed, Stuart began to recognize how gifted he was in one particular area and so concentrated more and more on just that one talent. He saw also that some of his other talents were in fact distractions that prevented him from pursuing this central interest. Consequently, he did better in his professional life. Although his marriage finally broke up, he survived it well enough to establish a reasonably stable liaison with another woman. The colleague who had referred him to me had feared that, should his marriage break up, he might commit suicide. In the event, however, he seemed to ride the storm quite well.

At this point in Stuart's treatment, I want to pause and examine the results so far. Two goals had been achieved: Stuart was better established in his professional life and was enjoying a high degree of satisfaction in it, and he had managed his domestic crisis better than had been expected. There are several factors to which one could attribute these results. During treatment, Stuart had gained sympathy for his early neglect by his mother and for the repeat of this neglect that his wife's affair symbolized. In my interpretations about his feeling that he did not have my attention, there was the implication that he *did* have my attention—that now he had an analyst–mother who was giving him attention. It would be possible to postulate that he had internalized a good figure who gave him attention and that this enabled him to give more attention to the talent in which he was truly gifted. It would also be possible to posit that the feeling of a good object attending to him enabled him to survive the rupture with his wife.

If the treatment had stopped at that point, I would have been asking myself some searching questions. Would this increased integration last—it seemed to be in place at the moment, but would it remain when treatment was finished? Even if it remained for a while, would it endure when the memory trace of the good object faded? In other words, has the good object, the experience of an attentive psychotherapist, been internalized and incorporated as a permanent structure? If there has not been such an internalization, has the basic structure of the self remained the same? And behind all this lies the vital question: what is the psychic act that engenders internalization?

In the word "understanding", there is the implication of a sympathetic togetherness with the patient's emotional perception of events.

The counterfeit cure

I think it would be difficult to find a more potent expression of what I call Cure through Understanding than Stuart's treatment, insofar as I have described it. There are, however, some worrying features that I shall try to explain. In the first case, have the psy-

chotherapist's sympathies been with the patient, against the wife?
If he had been treating the wife, would the sympathies be the
other way round? Is the psychotherapist subtly on the side of one
person against another, rather than on the side that is for truth
and against untruth? Is the cure based on an inner strength that is
in his permanent possession? Are we in the presence of maturity
or only its counterfeit?

Erich Fromm (1972, p. 74) defined a mature person as one who
is the subject of his own powers and therefore emancipated from
bondage to things and persons. While this bondage persists, the
person is immature or, to use Fairbairn's term, in a state of infantile dependence. The incestuous tie remains. The patient does not
evaluate the truth himself, but takes as the truth the perception of
things he shares with the psychotherapist. They share the same
outlook and so fulfil Fairbairn's definition of infantile dependence—in other words, a sameness of outlook of the child as of the
parent, or the patient as of the psychotherapist. The psychotherapist's job, however, is to avoid the patient becoming dependent
upon him: to foster the attachment is to enslave the patient further
within his infantile self. The question I raise is whether, in an
understanding mode of cure, the patient is being seduced into an
attachment to the psychotherapist instead of being emancipated
from the incestuous tie. Patients resist the process of emotional
growth and therefore try to manipulate psychotherapists into
maintaining the incestuous tie and not threatening it. There is also
the question here of whether the psychotherapist was offering
himself as a more appealing object than the wife and, as part of
that, offering a subtle alliance with the patient against the wife.

I want to return for a moment to Eric Fromm's definition of a
mature person—one who is the subject of his own powers and
who is able to own what he has done in the construction of his life.
There is the question as to whether, in a cure by understanding,
the psychotherapist has aided the struggle towards maturity or
sabotaged it. I want now to ask whether such a cure has equipped
the patient to manage adult challenges. There is a complex web of
challenges that makes up the pattern of adult life: the capacity to
bear loss, to mourn, to grieve, to bear disappointment, to bear
frustration, and to bear pain. We also need the capacity to withstand destructiveness in ourselves and in others, to bear envy and

jealousy in ourselves and in others, and to acknowledge our own deficiencies and consequently our own knowledge of ourselves. Does the cure we have been talking of enable us to own all this and to know it? The man who is mentally healthy is he who experiences himself as subject of his powers. The man who feels himself to be a victim, who feels that life has been unfair to him, has not achieved maturity. Would the cure by understanding free him from this bondage, would the mental attitude of victimhood be transformed into one of free subjectivity?

Achieving emotional security

Before returning to Stuart and continuing the sequel of events, I want to take two criteria that are, I believe, particularly good indicators of whether emotional maturity has been achieved. These are the capacity to bear criticism and the capacity to manage confrontation.

The person who cannot bear criticism seals himself off from an opportunity that is being offered for mental growth. No one likes criticism—it is painful and always touches on an area of personal deficiency of which we are ashamed or about which we possibly feel guilty. An inability to bear criticism paralyses growth. I knew someone who was so sensitive to criticism that as soon as she was criticized, she left her job. As you can imagine, she never kept a job for long and ended up unemployable. Such sensitivity combined with an inner or outer retreat also makes intimacy with another impossible. A marriage between two such individuals would constitute an alliance of two alienated people, wary of each other and keeping their emotional distance. I do not say that people like this do not survive, but mental health is concerned primarily with quality of life, not with survival. Such people manage to get by without committing suicide, but it is a question of getting *through* life, skirting along its edges, instead of *living* it.

The second criterion that indicates the achievement of emotional maturity is the capacity to manage confrontation. I knew someone who so hated confrontation that, rather than risk it, he would succumb to any proposal, however unfavourable it was to him and however antipathetic it was to his natural inclinations.

When asked why he had agreed to a suggestion, he would reply, "It was too impolite not to". He always gave in to another's point of view: on one occasion, he actually knew he was being cheated by an acquaintance who was selling him his second-hand car at an absurdly high price, but he purchased it rather than risk a confrontation. A person who cannot manage confrontation also has to skirt along the edges of life, usually envying those who grasp life and live it and thereby further aggravating his mental condition.

I have no doubt that a person feels very much better when he has experienced the sympathetic and intelligent understanding of another. If he chooses his niche in life carefully and steers a course so as to keep within it, then such a psychotherapeutic experience may protect him from mental breakdown in the future. There is, however, a "but". He may not be able to assimilate those adult challenges that are capable of so greatly expanding and deepening his capacity for love, joy, creativity, and self-knowledge, as well as his capacity to bear pain and suffering. I want now to return to our patient.

Knowledge and self-knowledge

I have mentioned that Stuart's capacity for work had become more focused and that he had survived the crisis of his marriage break-up. However, three important things remained unchanged: hatred for his brother, contempt for his father, and an attachment to his mother that was very sentimental in character. A resumé of a session follows.

> Although Stuart said he was feeling fine, some discordant facts soon came trickling through. He had had a row with his girlfriend, and he had received a letter from his wife's solicitor claiming a sum in alimony that would cripple him financially. I remarked on the way he felt the need to declare that he was feeling fine when in fact the truth was that disturbing happenings were bombarding him. He was playing out the role of little Stuart telling his Mummy–analyst that he was quite all right and had no problems. As all this unfurled in the session,

there was a touching pathos of this little boy needing to reassure his Mummy that he was all right and that she needn't trouble about him. There was still the feeling that he must keep all these painful things inside him and not burden others with them. I might have left things with that gentle understanding that existed between us undisturbed, had not hard questions confronted me. Why does he play out this role with me? Why does he pretend with the psychotherapist, the professional problem-solver, that he has no problems? So I made this interpretation: "You pretend to have no problems when, in truth, you have very big problems, because you are not generous enough to allow that this analyst might have the capacity to help not only Tony but you also."

The soft cradle of feelings was badly shaken by this interpretation. He muttered, spoke irritably, and when he left the session he banged the door, which he had not done before. The effect of that interpretation was that he spent the evening with Tony, his brother. In the course of conversation, he mentioned he was having psychotherapy, saying he had problems with which he needed help. Tony was greatly relieved to know that he was not the only one with problems, but he was also angry. He said that if my patient would only tell their mother, he would not feel so much like the family burden; by concealing his own problems, Stuart was adding to his, Tony's. Stuart did then tell his mother, and she was greatly relieved. She told Stuart how shut out she had always felt by him. The picture that then emerged was quite different from the one Stuart had initially sketched. It seemed he had aggravated his brother's emotional load and made his mother feel guilty that she had not mothered him better. Until this point, I had an understanding of him, but now I began to know him and he began to know himself also.

As he absorbed this self-knowledge, Stuart's relations with his family altered. He no longer hated his brother, and the sentimentality went out of his love for his mother. It did not happen all at once—it took a long time with many backslidings—but that interpretation was the beginning of it.

Some readers may want to challenge my evidence in connecting this interpretation with his initiation of a changed relationship with members of his family of origin. I can only say that I have had so many instances of such a change in direction following such an interpretation, both in my own practice and also in the experiences of people I have supervised, that it amounts to certainty on the principle of what John Henry Newman (1888) called "Proof through Convergence of Probabilities". A provisional acceptance—that this interpretation did set in train a series of emotional actions that began to make Stuart master of his own destiny—is needed in order to read on, because what follows is crucial to my thesis.

> When I made that interpretation, the emotional child I had in the consulting-room hated me. Stuart's hating did not last long, but it lasted long enough and it was definite enough to crack an inner illusory relationship that held his emotional self, a self that was struggling to escape its bondage but powerless to get out. When his hatred pushed that illusion out and left a space, his emotional self sprang into action. His hatred was now directed towards me (which I interpreted in many subsequent sessions), and he no longer enacted it towards his mother and brother. He took criticism from his brother and began to risk confrontation. This had a feedback effect that strengthened further his developing emotional self. My countertransference altered. Whereas before I had felt sorry for him, now I had respect for him. This respect was a reflection of his changed attitude towards his objects.

Permanent structural change in the personality occurs only when the patient himself initiates action. By action, I mean inner psychic action through which the individual brings himself into relation with real objects and not illusory objects that receive their colouring through a narcissistic investment from within. The mother who needed his self-sacrificing denial was a figment of Stuart's imagination—the real mother wanted to be a mother to him. This inner core of the self has the capacity for two actions: hating and loving. The beginning of a new structure began to occur with this patient when his hatred was mobilized against his inner paralysing illusion. It released love, experienced in the countertransference as respect: respect is the foundation stone without which love cannot be built.

A cure to last a lifetime

I now want to examine the question of whether the therapeutic endeavour prepares the patient for the crises of his future life. There is, of course, no insurance policy against what the future may bring and what events we shall be able to manage. It is, however, possible to compare a present emotional state with how it was previously. I have come across many patients who, having undergone therapy, cannot meet the two psychological criteria I set as indicators of emotional maturity, namely the capacity to receive criticism and the ability to manage confrontation. Such encounters happen so regularly that it has led me to some hard questioning of our therapeutic techniques. To me, one conclusion is incontrovertible: that if the patient is to manage the most severe crisis that life may bring, then the therapy itself must be a crisis. If it is a crisis—and a crisis that is survived—then the experience is a rich and deep one which acts as an inoculation against the patient's collapse in future crises. This conclusion needs closer examination.

In his paper "Formulating Interpretations in Clinical Psychoanalysis", John Klauber (1981b) says:

> Psychoanalysis has both traumatic and therapeutic elements. The clearest indication of its traumatic quality lies in the fact that it regularly induces a flight from reality. This is the most dramatic feature of analysis, and we describe it as the development of transference . . . I am sure that many psychoanalysts remember the experience of their ego being partially put out of action quite vividly from their own analysis. The traumatic power of analysis may be inferred from the patient's attempt to defend himself against the transference by projecting it into the outside world and trying to solve it there. A not infrequent example is by starting a sexual relationship at the beginning of analysis which may end as marriage as a

> defence against ending the analysis—that is, against the full
> power of the transference at all stages. [p. 112]

The inception of a treatment based on psychodynamic principles is a crisis—I am not saying that it *should* be a crisis but that it *is* one. It is my experience that psychotherapists and analysts frequently do not recognize this. We defend ourselves against the recognition because it is extremely frightening. Freud knew it, which is why he recommended that his analysands made no big life decisions while the analysis was in progress: he understood that it was an emotional trauma.

The usual story, however, is that we psychotherapists defend ourselves against knowledge of it because it is frightening. A woman in her 40s started analysis—a woman who had defiantly eschewed marriage. Within a fortnight of the analysis beginning, she declared that she was going to marry her current boyfriend—and stood by her declaration. It is frightening to realize that when a patient is in this hyperemotional state, the smallest word or action from the analyst can make a deep impression. I have supervised a fair number of people over the years, and, without doubt, what I have had to work at most is to extract from the material presented the evidence that illustrates the degree of the patient's emotional sensitivity to the psychotherapist's every word and action. As psychotherapists, we shrink from having to face up to the enormity of the emotional trauma that is set in train when a patient starts treatment.

What is so traumatic for the patient is that the knowledge of himself, which to date has lain hidden, is now to be revealed. Although it is a great relief when he comes into possession of that knowledge, he fights it off with all the power he can muster. He has organized his life on the basis of not knowing it, and now here comes this agent from Delphi to disrupt this state of affairs. I can remember learning something about myself in the first week of analysis that overthrew everything I had thought and believed. It took several years to come to terms with it. I had hitherto projected that aspect out of myself and attributed it to other people or organizations, but, of course, whenever someone gets rid of part of themselves in that way, they remain debilitated. The person needs that part of himself in order to be whole. I know that taking possession of that part of myself enabled me to manage and deal with certain life configurations that had not been possible for me before. All this is very fine, and it looks all right from the vantage point of hindsight, but most patients fight off self-knowledge. This fight can take many forms, but there is one common denominator: to persuade the psychotherapist to give up the pursuit of this knowledge. Deep down, however, the patient never forgives the psychotherapist if he reneges on what he has agreed to do. However, if the psychotherapist tries his utmost to be true to his task, the patient is enormously strengthened and has some equipment with which to counter the blows of outrageous fortune that may assail him in the future.

Conclusion

No analysis and no therapy can proceed without what I have referred to as Cure by Understanding—it is through this that the psychotherapist holds the patient while he dishes out the appalling medicine of self-knowledge. The understanding is a necessary part of the process, it is the servant of the process by which the patient comes to knowledge. But if understanding occurs with little or no knowledge, then I do not believe that the therapy has achieved a lasting change in character structure. What appears to be a cure is, in reality, a superficial appearance of well-being— underneath is still the infant unable to manage the crises of adult life.

Bion (1974) once said that, at the end of it all, the analyst's task was to introduce the patient to himself and that there has never been a man or woman who has come to knowledge of this sort without an unspeakable crisis (p. 90). I will end with the inscription at the head of a poem entitled "A Holocaust" by Francis Thompson (1913, p. 95; I understand the poet took the inscription from Coventry Patmore's *Religio Poetae*): "No man ever attained supreme knowledge unless his heart had been torn up by the roots".

CHAPTER NINE

The seductive psychotherapist

I once came across the following situation. Let us call the psychotherapist, Joseph, the patient, Patrick, and the patient's wife, Virginia.

Joseph had a reputation for being a kind and empathic psychotherapist. Patrick went to see him because he was suffering from severe obsessional symptoms. He had a fear of going blind which frequently reached panic proportions. In the initial interview, Joseph learned that Patrick was a librarian and was happily married with three children. In fact, his family seemed to be the happiest aspect of his life.

I will outline what began to take place, without going into the full details of this therapy. Patrick began to drop hints that he was not as happy with Virginia as he had made out in his initial interview. For instance, he let it drop that, when he came home at night from work, Virginia did not cook him a meal; that once, when they had planned to go out with the children and he arrived home a little late, Virginia had not waited for him but had just driven off; that when he got home and went to the fridge to get the beer that he was looking forward to, Virginia had already given it to a friend of hers. In addition to this, he began to hint that Virginia had homosexual leanings and wanted to spend more time with her friend, Fiona, than with himself. Every time that Patrick dropped one of these hints, Joseph was quickly on to it and got him to express the angry feelings he had towards his wife. Each time this happened, Joseph felt pleased that he was beginning to get Patrick to express his hostile feelings towards his wife. A situation developed where the marriage became more and more turbulent, and it also seemed that Virginia was spending more and more time with Fiona. As things worsened, Patrick's distress deepened to the point that Joseph felt that it was necessary to give him more substantial support. He suggested that Patrick take a firmer line with Virginia, and he increased Patrick's sessions from twice to three times a week. Eighteen months later, the marriage had broken up. Virginia had left to pursue her affair with Fiona, and an acrimonious legal case, which ended in divorce, soon followed.

Now the question I want to put is this: was it a good piece of therapy? The argument in favour might go something like this: the marriage was on the point of breaking down and the psychotherapist supported Patrick through its break-up, and if Joseph had not assisted Patrick through this painful process, he might have broken down. It is traumatic to go through a divorce in such circumstances.

I want now to describe another very similar case, in which the psychotherapist related to the patient in quite a different way. In this case, the psychotherapist was called Thomas, the patient was called Peter, and Peter's wife was called Patricia.

In the initial interview, Peter described to Thomas some very severe obsessional symptoms. For instance, he had to wash his hands about six times an hour, and he had to check and recheck whether he had turned off the gas stove at home. He also declared that his marriage was fine, and he gave Thomas the impression of being a thoroughly nice guy.

In the initial interview, Peter began to describe how afflicted he was with his obsessions. In about the fifth session, however, he alluded to Patricia not letting him go to bed when he was tired. In the session after that, he let drop that Patricia had gone off to a dinner party without him. Thomas did not say anything the first time, but the second time set him thinking. He wondered why Patricia went off to a dinner party without Peter and whether Peter was doing something to anger Patricia. Thomas contented himself with remarking, "It seems that Patricia was very angry with you". At this, Peter gave a jerk of his head and began to talk about a colleague at work who did not recognize the hard work he put in. Thomas then observed that he had been annoyed by his remark. This brought from Peter the bitter retort, "I thought you were on my side". Thomas replied that it seemed he had come to enlist his support against his wife. At this, Peter protested and said that he loved his wife. However, Thomas pursued the matter. He said it seemed to be the case, nevertheless, that Patricia was angry. He further observed that Peter was angry with him whenever he didn't support him, and this led him to wonder whether Peter got angry when anyone else didn't support his point of view. This brought an interesting revelation that had not emerged before. Peter told Thomas that he was a committed socialist and that Patricia persisted in being an indulged conservative. He went on to say that she came from the landed gentry and had always been very spoiled.

Of necessity, I must condense what occurred but, briefly, Thomas pointed out in this and in subsequent sessions that unless Peter got backing for his own point of view he became sulky and bad-tempered. He asked Peter to consider whether this in itself was not a big indulgence on his part: that he had always gathered around him people who supported his view of things. Thomas said to him one day that he was rather like a little boy who becomes very sulky when Mummy doesn't give him exactly what he wants the moment he wants it. Following all this, Peter revealed that when he first came to see Thomas, his marriage had been in a very poor state, but that over the last few weeks it had improved greatly. At the end of eighteen months, the marriage was not only intact but, on Peter's own assertion, was much happier than ever before. Both his obsessions had also cleared up considerably.

Different styles, different outcomes

Now I think you will agree that the results of these two pieces of therapy were very different. To return to the first case, Patrick still had most of his anxieties at the end of the therapy, and, what is more, a couple of years later he sought therapy again. In the second case, Peter did not need to return for more therapy—his marriage was happy and remained undisrupted. Now you will notice that two very different styles of therapy were operating: I believe that the two very different outcomes were a consequence of those styles. I want now to look at the difference between the two therapeutic approaches and why the outcomes differed.

On the face of it, Joseph was being kind and sympathetic in his treatment of Patrick, but I think one would have to say that he was not psychologically very shrewd. When Joseph listened to Patrick relating the incidents where his wife had been negligent towards him, he did not ask himself whether Patrick was really revealing the moody and controlling behaviour against which his wife was reacting—it is usually the case that, when someone is exceedingly guilty about something, he has great difficulty in revealing it. There is such a powerful fear of retaliation from the psychotherapist, that all he can do is hint at it. So Patrick was hinting that he had done something that had contributed, or may have contributed, to Virginia's behaviour. When Joseph sympathized with Patrick and, in effect, said to him, "Poor fellow, I understand how you feel", unconsciously that was received by Patrick as a message telling him that Joseph sympathized with him because he, Joseph, was also tortured by a wife like Virginia. So Patrick and Joseph get into a homosexual huddle against these persecuting wives, and hence Virginia, perhaps not sensibly but on the principle of the law of talion, does a tit-for-tat and gets into a homosexual huddle with Fiona against the two men. Again, I stress that this is a condensation.

There is no doubt that when Peter said that his marriage was much improved, it had a direct relation to the way that Thomas was treating him. What Thomas did was to confront Peter with this sulky little-boy attitude of his, with his indulged self, this feeling-sorry-for-himself attitude. Peter, of course, became annoyed when Thomas pointed this out, but he came to recognize the truth of it. At that moment, something happened.

Such an act of emotional insight is an active process, just as the physical act of seeing is. In other words, the moment of recognition represents an inner act of self-possession. A person takes it in and no longer disowns it, he no longer pushes it out. If somebody upsets me or does something that is not to my liking and I pout and get moody, the people around me react to my behaviour. I may be totally unconscious of what I'm doing, though it is quite obvious to other people. (This was, in fact, the very way in which Freud went about inferring the existence of an Unconscious.) If, on the other hand, I am aware of the little kid in myself who gets bad-tempered when he doesn't get his own way, and I can smile at this side of myself, then it is socially a very different matter. I contain this side of me within me rather than discharging it into the social atmosphere. I want to stress that I am not talking of conscious control where I make an effort to contain my reactions but a quite natural spontaneous situation where there is a child within me that is contained. In the case of Peter, perhaps the only thing he might have been aware of was a reluctant acceptance of what Thomas said to him.

I think you will see that the two different results, then, were direct consequences of the two different modes of therapy. Joseph was seductive. Although one may feel that this is a harsh word to use, I think it is the word that is most apposite. Joseph sympathized with Patrick, which means that he did not ask himself the question that Thomas did. He therefore colluded with his patient *against* the third party who, in this case, was Patrick's wife, Virginia. Essentially, what Joseph did not do, but Thomas did, was to invite the patient to confront something within himself. I am not saying, though, that Virginia was not reacting to Patrick in a childish way—most of us marry partners at our own level of emotional development. What I am saying, however, is that when something in the patient is challenged and the patient confronts it, this challenge is then passed on to the spouse. My experience is that if the psychotherapist conducts himself in the way that Thomas did, then the spouse usually rises to the challenge, just as Peter did with Thomas. Therapy then is a catalyst within an ecological niche. This niche is the micro-interactional environment.

An element, then, in seductiveness is one party joining forces with another *against* a third party. I believe that therapy conducted in this way is ultimately damaging. Many patients, as is clear in both these cases, scoop their psychotherapist, often in the most subtle ways, into such an alliance, and the psychotherapist can, like Joseph, be quite unaware of it.

Conclusion

I want to conclude with a question. Which of these two outcomes is the better? It is, I believe, an extraordinarily important question, because if the second outcome, other things being equal, is considered the better one, then to conduct therapy in Joseph's mode is destructive. If, on the other hand, you think the Joseph/Patrick outcome the most favourable, then to conduct therapy in the mode of Joseph may earn high praise from you.

I think certain conclusions are unavoidable. The first is that value judgements are inherent in the psychotherapeutic process—neutrality is a myth. The second conclusion is that the stance that the psychotherapist takes has a formative result upon the patient's resulting situation in life. Psychotherapists *do* something—we cannot shirk responsibility for our patients' outcomes. Some situations are too difficult for us; in others, we are tricked. It is important to know our limitations when we attempt this work. I believe, however, that the seductive psychotherapist does not strengthen character, and strengthening character should be one of our aims, to help our patients meet the crises of life and the suffering with which life unavoidably presents us. If we fail in this, I believe we fail very badly. We are not trying to protect our patients from the pain of life—we are trying to strengthen them, so that they can manage the worst.

CHAPTER TEN

Mimesis in narcissistic patients

In this chapter, I intend to study one mode of action which is characteristic of narcissistic patients. I have called this mode of action *mimesis*. Natural historians use the term to describe the way in which one animal copies another; art historians use it to describe ornament that mimics materials or forms of a previous age. In both cases, although the essence of the two substances is different, the secondary qualities are similar. The purpose of the mimicry is deception—the Asilid fly mimics the bee in an attempt to avoid its predators; the laminex tabletop in a canteen displays the grain lines of wood, so diners feel they are eating fine food while seated at a wooden table.

The mode of investigation

The transference is the instrument that a psychoanalyst uses to investigate the inner structure of the personality. The transference means the emotional structure of relating that the patient adopts towards the analyst, and it is the instrument that the analyst uses to research the inner structure of the personality. Such usage only makes sense if we claim that the structure of the relationship between patient and analyst reflects a relationship between different parts of the self in the inner world.

The claim is that the many-faceted bondings that fashion the totality of what transpires between analyst and patient are themselves expressions of the relations between different parts of the self. It was Jung (1935) who first gave clear expression to the view that the self is not a whole but an amalgam of many personalities within the boundaries of one person. At that time, Jung called each of these personalities "complexes". Jung had the view that mental health depended upon the psyche's capacity to integrate these varied complexes.

The analyst uses the transference to make inferences about the way in which the parts of the self relate to each other. He also uses it to scrutinize the modes of action operating between these parts. Clinical observation convinces me that intentional aim exists in these different parts and that these are frequently at variance with each other. I follow Edmund Husserl (1973, p. 73) in thinking that the ego is always an active agent. The ego always consents to receive an impression. In the case of a negative hallucination, it vetoes such a consent. I would add to what Husserl has said, and say that within the personality there are many such egos. Within self psychology, practitioners tend to avoid the term "ego". I prefer to call the active self "the ego" and retain the term "self" as the same entity but as the receiver of impressions. This corresponds to George Herbert Mead's (1972, pp. 173–178) way of distinguishing between the self looked at from the aspect of the I and the me. Severe trauma makes an impression upon the self, but the way this occurs depends upon the intentional actions of the egos. To define the matter, I would state that the ego gives form to the self impressions.

In this chapter, I describe as best I can those patients who demonstrate mimetic characteristics; I then try to draw inferences. With such patients, my aim is to grasp the inner personality structure, and the result is a model that I have found helpful both in understanding and in treating them. I now wish to introduce a particular form of transference delusion, albeit a well-hidden one. The delusion is the product of the patient psychologically having inserted himself in another, and he frequently panics when an analyst begins to uncover this fact. The situation is aided by the patient's control of the analyst through guilt. I think this explains Wilfrid Bion's comment to a patient: "But I am not trying to help you" (cited in Gosling, 1980). That would have been the truth, but the patient stimulates the analyst's superego: "After all, surely I should be trying to help my patients?" I want first to examine how matters appear to the patient and then how the analyst experiences this phenomenon.

A patient in a mimetic transference

The patient admires his analyst and believes he has a special right to him and that the analyst has a special love for him, the patient. Sometimes such a patient believes that he is the analyst's chosen interpreter. If his analyst is criticized by another, he becomes paranoid. At the same time, he is ashamed of being a patient, and, in extreme cases, this can even lead to violence. The power of such a transference may last for more than a decade after the analysis ends and frequently remains an integral part of the patient's emotional orientation for the rest of his life. If the analyst is famous, such a patient may become known as the analyst's editor, executor, and chosen interpreter of his works. There are cases, for instance, where in an edition of the analyst's letters, those passages that reflect unfavourably on him are strictly censored. Any negativity about the analyst is admitted with difficulty and is usually qualified in such a way as to lose any force.

There is another occurrence that is also a familiar drama in psychoanalytic societies. It is the faithful disciple who suddenly turns viciously against his analyst. From having been a devoted son or daughter, the patient, usually some few years after the analysis is finished, does a violent volte-face and turns on his analyst—there is nothing too bad that can be said about him. Perhaps a classic case of this would be Paula Heimann's violent repudiation of her analyst, Melanie Klein, having once been her most devoted champion. An example of lesser violence was Ferenczi's estrangement from Freud. The loyal disciple and the violent rebel are, however, two sides of the same coin. In both, a moment of freedom is shunned. In such a moment, the individual stands on his own authority, with no guarantor assuring him of his rightness; he stands unprotected inwardly and outwardly. It is a moment that is frightening in the extreme. It is, I believe, what Bertrand Russell (1971) was talking about when he referred to "that terrible loneliness in which one shivering consciousness looks over the rim of the world into the cold unfathomable abyss" (p. 15). It is this moment that is avoided through mimetic action.

The analyst's perspective

Having discussed how observers see a patient in a mimetic transference and how the patient experiences the matter, I now turn to look at it from the analyst's point of view.

The problems mimesis presents

Some psychotherapists are satisfied with a cure based on the consolidation of a mimetic transference, and to them a loyal disciple, far from being a problem, may even be encouraged. However, these remarks are addressed to those analysts and psychotherapists who perceive it as a problem. What is the experience of such an analyst? Probably the most salient feature in the communications of such a patient is an absence of genuineness; this is close to falseness but places emphasis on what is missing. This lack of genuineness flows from the patient's intense anxiety to be "in" the emotional attitude of the analyst and not to be discordant with it. The patient hastens to be in agreement with what the analyst says. But it does not stop there, because when the patient is driven by intense anxiety, pressure is put upon the analyst's superego to conform to an image that the patient wants. In other words, the patient attempts to merge with the ideals of the analyst. So, for instance, if that ideal is to promote a more humane attitude within psychiatry, the patient will insert himself into it. If the analyst has a deep-seated belief in psychoanalysis, then the patient will insert himself into that ideal. I believe that such a patient demands a technique of the analyst which, by definition, cannot be taught. The only technique that undermines this kind of defence is an inner search for self-knowledge.

Frequently, things the analyst has said are repeated back to him within a short period of time. These statements have not been digested but *ingested* and reflected back. On careful examination, it can be seen that such a "report back" follows a break in treatment or a failure on the part of the analyst to be in touch with the emotional core of the patient. The clue in this is that it reflects an emotional state that is a reaction—and not a response—to something that the analyst has done or failed to do. It requires time and careful observation to monitor the trigger.

Treatment of mimetic patients

It seems clear from what I am saying that the analyst's only method of treating such a patient is to know his own feelings and his own thoughts, as opposed to what he believes he ought to feel or think. There is big trouble if he believes that he feels or thinks something when he does not, because then a situation can arise where there is no way of stopping mimesis. What occurs, then, is the state of affairs that Jung (1935, pp. 140–141) called *participation*. It is extremely important for those treating mimetic patients, and their supervisors, to distinguish between feelings that are real and feelings that are sentimental. The inner difference between the two is enormous, though outwardly they appear similar. Where the patient is in the mimetic situation, the feelings are also a mimic—false or sentimental. Real feelings grasp "hard and stubborn facts", to use a phrase of William James, but sentimental feelings are fantasy productions. I believe that a careful diagnosis of the difference between these two entities is essential for those engaged in psychotherapy.

The prime desire of a patient in the mimetic transference, then, is to be "in" the emotional ideal of the analyst. He cannot get into the emotional core of another, as this holy of holies allows of no such entry. There is a deep-seated belief that the analyst is in love with his own reflection into which the patient desperately tries to insert himself.

I once had a crude and somewhat pathetic example of this. I was treating a narcissistic girl with severe obsessional symptoms who worked as a secretary. Then she became obsessed with the idea of studying psychology and started to go to evening classes to study it. Her obsessional anxiety intensified. She knew I was a psychologist. At the right moment I said to her, "You believe that I have fallen in love with my own reflection and that I will only love you if you become a psychologist like me". After that, she gave up psychology. Although she became more relaxed, a deeper identification remained and was only partially resolved.

Other phenomena that the analyst can observe are as follows. Moments of hostility erupt. Sometimes they may slip out in an undertone; at other times they erupt more violently, only to disappear. A psychoanalyst told me that he was once treating a submissive adolescent. One day, in the middle of a compliant sentence, a voice came out of him which said, "I'd like to murder you". He then continued with his sentence as if there had been no interruption. It was as if this voice had come from a separate person buried in the depths. Sometimes other phenomena whose source is in a dissociated part are displayed in violent actions outside the consulting-room: a car crash before or after a session; a violent row with a workmate, spouse, or parents; or an alcoholic binge. At first, there seems to be no connection between such happenings and the course of the analysis, but the repetition of such incidents justifies the conclusion that they are reactions to the actions of the analyst. For instance, a young man used to say to me that he enjoyed dropping in for a chat each week, but, at each break in treatment, he became drunk and violent. He was highly intelligent and came to the conclusion himself that these violent outbreaks had to be connected with the breaks in treatment. All these phenomena are in contrast to the compliant behaviour in the consulting-room.

Behaviour of mimetic types

Another aspect of the clinical picture in such cases is the way the patients function professionally. They frequently hold down responsible jobs and superficially appear mature, but if they are of the mimetic type their abilities are inadequate for the job. In spite of intensive interview and selection procedures, it is not picked up, and it causes intense frustration in other people in the organization, especially, as frequently happens, when they hold an important post. Within a year of the person holding the job, it becomes evident that he cannot manage it, and the other staff members become exasperated. I think that it is often the case that such people are of this mimetic type. They are so finely tuned to what is wanted by their interviewers that they pass through the selection procedure, but, within a year, it becomes clear they cannot make autonomous decisions. There is also a characteristic mode of referral when these people are referred for psychotherapy—they are referred not because they "need treatment" but just because they need a little "supportive counselling".

In my last year in London before migrating to Australia, I did not take on any new patients for analysis or long-term psychotherapy. People knew I was available for brief work, assessments, or supportive counselling, so I was asked if I would mind "seeing Mrs X and give her a little support because her daughter is recovering from a nervous breakdown". It did not take long for Mrs X to reveal the appalling emotional abyss in her home life. Tragedy struck when her daughter threw herself in front of a train, and then, on receiving the news, her husband had a coronary and died. The mimetic transference was symbolically illustrated in this case: the distraught woman wanted to buy and then occupy the house we were vacating when we left London. The clue to the intense things that are happening in the emotional field of force is to understand the enacted happenings as symbolic of internal desire.

Although I believe that mimesis is a crucial part of the clinical picture in these cases, providing us with clues about the pathology, this mimetic element seems frequently to be missed. The patient lives by incorporating the emotional imago of the analyst or psychotherapist as his own persona. In the absence of an individuated functioning ego, he lives *through* another's ego-action. Such a person has lived on this basis: he has a very highly developed faculty for cognizing the emotional orientation of another.

In London, I was supervising an Englishwoman who had a Turkish boyfriend. The Londoner she was treating dreamt of his psychotherapist bending over an atlas with her finger pointing to Turkey. If this had been an isolated instance in the treatment, she might have dismissed it, but it happened again and again. Her patient's ability to cognize the important foci of her emotional life was uncanny and it unnerved her. She once said to me, "I feel he has got right inside me".

The type of passion that drives a person into another is well described in the madness that gripped Charles Arrowby in that haunting novel of Iris Murdoch's *The Sea, The Sea*, where he is determined to take possession of Hartley, a flame from his youth.

I hope it is now clear that we are dealing here with profound emotional disturbance. It is a disturbance that is on the increase and one that is extremely difficult to treat. We also need to ask why such people come for treatment—as I have said, they frequently avoid asking for it directly, but why do they come even indirectly? I think the answer to this may emerge more clearly when we have examined the inner structure of such patients.

A model of the mind

I now turn from the description of phenomena to make inferences about the structure of the individual's self and the origins of the state of mimesis.

The structure of the self

The first inference I make is that the self of the patient is in a state of disunity and disintegration. This means that co-ordinated action is not possible. Shame is the emotional registration of this inner disunion (this is well described by Dietrich Bonhoeffer in his book *Ethics*: 1970, pp. 24–25). From shame, I infer this inner disunion. The mimetic thrust means that the patient's ego is unable in itself to be a source of action, so it has to live within another.

The Asilid fly mimics the bee because it lacks the effectiveness of the bee itself.

A conclusion can be drawn from this, and that is that the self becomes passive. Passivity is that psychological state in which the self is the object. It has to generate action from outside itself and achieves this through an eroticization of the self. The eroticization is what fuels the disunited self. When that "fuel" runs out, a re-eroticization has to take place. I think it likely that the point at which a patient approaches an analyst or psychotherapist is the moment when eroticization can no longer be maintained.

The eroticized self incorporates entities that function like masturbatory instruments, not for the body but for the self. These instruments, which can be human figures, are incorporated to motivate the self and may be used to soothe, caress, attack, or blame. These actions eroticize the self. A system gets set up whereby all action then becomes geared to eroticizing the self. This becomes the goal of human action. Actions may appear exemplary, but again they are mimics. Their internal structure is quite different. The pragmatist says that, if a social action is effective, it makes no difference what its inner structure consists of. I think that social psychologists need to do more work on this issue. When humans function for the disunited self in this way, the secret power being thus exercised in itself operates as an eroticizing agent.

The disunited self's problem, which it has to solve, is how to generate action. Only an integrated self is able to be the source of its own action. The eroticized self incorporates a series of images that flatter the self into action, but these images are dependent upon regular reinforcement from outside. The outer figures then function as auxiliary egos. The individual's psychological life depends entirely upon them—many extremely gifted people do not achieve creative synthesis, because they are crippled by mimesis. However, true creative activity flows from what is really "me".

The other inference I make is that what is manifest outwardly is symbolic of the inner state of the self. Therefore, the creative individual part of the self is enslaved to another part that is cruel and savage. In the mimetic transference, the manifest part of the self that mimics the emotional attitudes of the analyst is the part that is enslaved to the savage tyrant that does all in his power to remain hidden. It is also this hidden tyrant that possesses the agent part of the self. The personality, then, is in need of this part of the self, but there is great resistance to letting it be flushed out into the light of day. Yet when it is, great benefits accrue to the person.

> I once had a woman in treatment who was submissive to her husband, who was a brute. His contempt of her was extreme, and her submission to him was sickening to witness. However, a ruthless ogre that held her captive within was at last smoked out of his den into the daylight. This event in the treatment coincided with her standing up to her husband for the first time.

This particular aspect of therapeutic technique was understood best by Fairbairn, who saw the task as the release of bad inner objects. Although it was central to his description of the therapeutic task, especially with schizoid patients, and although he has been adopted widely in the States and certainly influenced Kohut, this core understanding of his has not been adopted. I believe the reason for this is that Fairbairn's (1976) model implies that an individual has rightful claims on another (pp. 62–70). Mullen (1991) makes the same point in a paper he wrote in which he contests the view that jealousy need not necessarily be described as pathological: a person could be rightfully jealous. I can make a claim on my neighbour: this value has its foundation in the inner personality structure such as I have been trying to describe.

How such a personality is constructed

I want now to turn to the reason why a personality should have become inwardly constructed in the way I have been describing. I should dearly love to examine the cultural reasons, but that is another subject. There is no doubt that this personality type has increasingly drawn the attention of psychoanalysts. What are the origins of such a construction? I certainly do not know the answer, but I have observed certain concomitant phenomena that may possibly put us on a track worthy of examination. Patients of this type whom I have treated have had a traumatic childhood—either there had been a psychotic mother, a delinquent father, a death of one or both parents, the death of a close sibling during infancy, or they lived in a time of great social upheaval. The analyst or psychotherapist then may conjecture that the infant has been subjected to pain that is unbearable. Here is another inference: that intense pain lasting a sufficient time breaks the self into pieces. My evidence for this is that when integration of parts occurs in treatment, the pain is well-nigh unbearable. This raises a very important ethical issue: is it right to expose a patient to such pain if it is more than can be borne? The answer to this depends on one's view of what happens to pain that cannot be borne psychologically. I have no doubt that such a patient cannot be successfully treated without a degree of pain that is an outrage to even the most hard-hearted. I once found it difficult even to be the emotional onlooker of such pain, and to be the bearer of it oneself is far worse. A patient once said to me, "Such pain as this is obscene".

A further question arises as to why the parts break up in such a way that certain parts are held captive by another. I believe that there is a multifaceted answer to this. What the tyrant part of the personality proscribes is any development. True development cannot occur without pain, without a return to the point where the fragmentation took place. The tyrant guards the fortress. The other fragments of the self are under contract to the tyrant. The benefit of such an arrangement is protection against pain; the deficit is renunciation of the self as source of action. It is a self structured in this way that has to resort to mimesis.

Conclusion

In E. M. Forster's *A Passage to India* (1924, p. 263), Dr Assiz said, "There are many ways of being a man", and he went on to define his own unique way of being a man. With all the mimetic patients I have encountered, a moment has occurred when it has been as clear as daylight that the individual has opted for the mimetic stance. I doubt whether this option was available in infancy, but opportunities to renew the option occur in the course of treatment.

Is any way of being a man acceptable? To be a Hitler is obviously not acceptable. It is clear that all societies revolt against particular ways of being a man, although the bounds of tolerance vary considerably from one society to another. Is there anything wrong with the mimetic personality? Is not such a person free to live in that particular way? Among the numerous people who never present themselves to a psychotherapist or analyst, the question does not arise. I have never had a patient who has presented himself directly because of the mimetic problem. However, these patients often come to the analyst when they are near disaster point—they are finally confronting the moral dilemma of mimesis. They come because they are wayworn and battered by the hammerings of their social intimates. I believe that it is only by understanding the inner structure that it is possible for a psychotherapist to treat these patients successfully.

CHAPTER ELEVEN

Narcissism

T his chapter is based on two papers, entitled "Narcissism and Feelings" and "Narcissistic Patients, The Problems for a Psychotherapy Unit". Each paper examined different aspects of narcissism, so the text of each has been retained in order to develop these aspects fully. There is inevitably some overlap and repetition of material between sections, and some material repeats text written earlier in this book.

Narcissism and feelings

It is possible for me to feel better for several different reasons. I may be very distressed because a close friend of mine has died, but if another friend takes me out to dinner, or I go out on a boat on the Harbour when it is bathed in perfect sunlight, I may feel better. A sympathetic friend may talk to me, and I will be able to speak to him about the circumstances that led up to my friend's death. On the other hand, I may feel dejected, not because a friend has died, but, for no reason that I can identify, I might just feel down. If this state of affairs goes on for some time and I cannot discover in any way what the reason for it is, I may decide to approach a psychiatrist.

The psychiatrist may make a diagnosis and tell me that I am depressed. He may prescribe some antidepressants, and I may feel better after I have taken the prescribed dosage for some time. Towards the latter part of the last century, a psychiatrist (or alienist, as they used to be called) might have recommended that I go away for a holiday, visit a famous spa, and take the waters. If I was lucky, I might end up feeling better.

The psychiatrist may, on the other hand, recommend that I visit him twice a week for psychotherapy. I do not know what this is, but I do as he has asked, and he listens with sympathy to what I have to say. He is a very understanding person and makes various comments that demonstrate both his understanding and his goodwill. After some weeks, I begin to feel considerably better. However, two years later, I again lapse into depression. From the psychiatrist's point of view, the therapy had been successful in that it gave me two years of relief from my depressed condition. Perhaps the best that he hoped for was to give me temporary relief. But is it too ambitious to expect anything better than this? Would it be realistic to expect to be able to give someone permanent relief for emotional distress?

What constitutes psychoanalysis?

Over the last 10 years, I have seen many patients who had been treated previously by either psychotherapists or psychoanalysts, and it has been clear that the treatment had only been capable of giving temporary relief. Karl Abraham (1973) believed that the advantage psychoanalysis has over other forms of therapy (and he was talking in the 1920s) is that psychoanalysis is capable of giving permanent relief from a patient's emotional disorder. Another way of putting this is to say that Abraham believed that it is possible to bring about permanent changes in the inner mental constitution.

There is a common element in the diverse therapeutic nostrums that are offered to a patient: the holiday at a spa, the antidepressant, taking the waters, a course of psychotherapy—all are dependent upon an external object or phenomenon for the relief of emotional suffering. Now you may argue that this is not the case with psychotherapy, because the act of understanding transforms an outer object into an inner possession. My answer to this lies in Abraham's thesis and what he meant by psychoanalysis. We may be sure that he did not mean that the practitioner was a member of the International Psychoanalytical Society, or that a patient attends for psychoanalysis five times a week, or that the patient lies on the couch. These things in themselves do not constitute what he meant by psychoanalysis. Similarly, there could be a therapeutic procedure in which, although there were many acts of understanding on the patient's part, they would not constitute a procedure that could be defined as psychoanalysis or even as a therapy that was derived from psychoanalysis.

Now I want to give you a small piece of interaction between a psychotherapist and a patient to illustrate what I mean.

A patient came to see me because he had suffered from depression for many years, if not for his entire life. Unusually for him, he was once late for a session. He came in dejected and lifeless and started talking about his sister who had always had much more of his mother's attention than he had. Now, I knew that as he had left the consulting-room after the previous session, he had seen another patient, a woman. It was unusual for this to happen as, in the normal course of events, he did not encounter other patients of mine either on his way in or on his way out. When he started talking about his mother's attention being directed to his sister, it seemed obvious for me to say: "You have come late today. I notice that your tone is a bit dejected and your general demeanour is one where you are feeling rather hopeless. Yet, when I saw you three days ago, you were hopeful and confident and said that you felt that the therapy had brought considerable benefits." I paused for a moment. He just said rather peremptorily, "Yes, I was feeling better when I was here on Monday", and then lapsed into silence. I said, "I think the trigger for this changed state of mind was when you saw a woman coming into this building as you were leaving after the Monday session. It gave you a sudden jerk when you realized that I had turned my attention to Mary" (Mary was his sister's name). He looked up with a bit of spark in his face and said that he had not seen the woman before. I replied, "I think it has been some time since you've seen another patient of mine, and you had become a lulled into the idea that I did not have any other patients and that you were my sole charge, as it were". His response was: "I always hated it when my mother spent nearly all her time with Mary."

Now, I wonder if you can see anything wrong with that exchange, that piece of interaction. Perhaps "wrong" is not the right word—was it okay? Would it have been satisfactory to conclude that episode by going on to say that it must have been awful for him to have had his mother so taken up with his sister? A great deal of therapy is, in fact, conducted along the lines of that vignette, and to have concluded the episode in such a way would have been quite typical. Had I said that, the patient would, I believe, have felt he had a sympathetic listener and had found a psychotherapist who understood him. The psychotherapist has entered into the patient's inner perspective, and the patient feels better for it.

The experience of the Other

I am quite sure that no therapy can succeed unless the psychotherapist manages to see things from the patient's point of view, but if he sees things *only* from the patient's point of view, the therapy will lack an essential ingredient—the experience of the Other.

The psychotherapist

If the psychotherapist puts himself entirely into the shoes of the patient and bases his understanding on the patient's own point of view, excluding all else, he will do nothing to solve the patient's basic problem. The patient came to the psychotherapist in the first place because his own point of view had not solved his problem. To be able to solve it, he needs the point of view of the Other.

Returning to the interaction described above, imagine for a moment this patient's mother when he was a little child. Imagine him demanding his mother's attention all the waking hours of the day, so that whenever his mother turned her attention to his sister, he started to scream. You can imagine his mother shouting, "Can't you leave me alone for a moment!" or "You expect me to have my eyes on you every moment of the day!" Now you might say that a reasonable mother should have sat down and rationally discussed things with her child. However, I am not sure I have met a mother like that, because mothers are like all of us—irascible, driven to the point of despair, and so on. I am not saying the mother *was* like this, but the psychotherapist needs to have the Other, the mother, in his perspective. Taking it further, imagine an absurd scene where one patient demands all the psychotherapist's attention. The psychotherapist acquiesces to his demands and gets rid of a woman patient who annoys him. However, the patient finds out that the psychotherapist has another patient and is dissatisfied, so the psychotherapist gets rid of that other patient as well. And, bit by bit, week by week, he gets rid of all his other patients. But the patient is not even satisfied with this and demands that the psychotherapist get rid of his wife and family. Finally, the psychotherapist ends up in an isolated *folie à deux*, alone with the patient.

The patient

There is one very significant aspect of narcissism that we need to take account of. In the popular way of looking at things, we often tend to believe that narcissism is commensurate with a robust self. But this is not the case. You imagine someone who is very narcissistic as always talking about himself, being very self-inflated, always wanting to be the centre of attention, believing he can do something better than anyone else, and so on. With such a person, you may draw the conclusion that the person's self is in good order, but you would be wrong. In fact, what we discover in someone who is very narcissistic is that there is almost an entire obliteration of his own self. There is a way of looking at this phenomenon which can be helpful and, I believe, accurate. The Other symbolizes the self, which means that the person who pushes all others out of his inner social arena is pushing out his own true self. To the extent that the grandiose self flourishes, the true self is suppressed, if not annihilated.

You are probably all aware of the distinction that Winnicott (1960a) made between the true self and the false self. In this case, the person who is filling all the social space with his own importance or vanity is totally, or almost totally, suppressing the true self. In other words, the narcissistic display is the false self that is obliterating the person's own centre from which mental health proceeds.

There is something else that goes with this condition. Beneath the external display, the narcissistic person is extremely self-denigrating. The version of this that we often meet in psychotherapy is the person who denigrates himself. It may look as if he is humble and self-deprecating, but grandiosity lies at the base of it. If you think about it for a moment, you will realize that a self-denigrating preoccupation with oneself is, ultimately, focusing attention on oneself to the exclusion of others. As Freud said in "Mourning and Melancholia" (1917e [1915]), he discovered that if he agreed with the self-accusations of a patient, the patient got furious.

Obliteration of the psychotherapist

I want you to look upon what I have been saying in this light. Consider the psychotherapist who is empathizing with the patient's point of view almost entirely and, in the process, obliterating himself. The patient is thereby deprived of any experience of the Other, and his own narcissistic state is endorsed and supported. There are two components to this. First, it may be that the psychotherapist is himself narcissistic; second, the patient's own narcissism has obliterated the psychotherapist's true self in the interaction. Now I do not think that it is a question of either/ or; what usually occurs is a combination of both. That is, the narcissistic currents in the psychotherapist's own mental life and those currents in the patient combine to obliterate the true self of the psychotherapist. My experience tells me that this is a very common state of affairs. When I first started work as a psychotherapist, my own narcissism contributed to a kind of self-annihilation when I was engaged in psychotherapeutic treatment. But I have also heard examples of it in a great number of clinical presentations from psychotherapists and analysts of all different schools of clinical thought.

> I will give you an example of what I mean. When I was in London, I was once supervising a psychotherapist who was a Scotswoman with a very strong Scottish accent. She was seeing for treatment a very flamboyant and self-opinionated man. During one session, this man said, "I have always thought Scots people are very inferior to the English". And he went on to speak in a very disparaging way of a Scotsman he knew and how stupid he was, even copying his accent at one point. I might mention that this was not the only time when he made a remark of this sort—he did so quite frequently. I asked the psychotherapist what she felt when her patient was making these derogatory remarks about Scots people. She replied that she thought he was trying to express his feeling of inferiority. When I asked her what she had felt herself, she reiterated her earlier comment. So I said, "Say you went to a party and found yourself talking to a man and he said that the Scots were an inferior race. What would you feel?" She replied immediately, "I would feel most indignant".

Why did she not feel indignant when this man said the same thing to her in the psychotherapeutic setting? What had occurred that her own sense of worth had become inaccessible? I can only think of one answer, and that is that her own narcissism has been channelled into the psychotherapeutic procedure. Her own narcissism—that aspect of it that obliterated her true self—had been stimulated in the session so that her own true self had become

entirely annihilated. It meant that this therapy was being conducted in such a way that, from the patient's point of view, the
other person was being emotionally obliterated. That person, the
psychotherapist, went along with it.

The result of this situation is that the patient's own inner self-
denigrating force, that which is suppressing his own true self and
inner sense of self-respect, is not being challenged. In such a case,
the therapy ends with the patient feeling better and being grateful
to the psychotherapist. But, alas, the narcissism in the patient remains untouched. The patient experiences temporary relief, but
then his problems surface again and the emotional disorder re-
turns—because it is founded upon narcissism. So the problems
with which he came will surface again. It is as I was saying in the
beginning: the patient feels better because he has had a sympathetic listener, but that feeling of relief is and remains dependent
upon an outer figure being sympathetic. The inner state and the
structure that constitutes it do not change in the slightest.

The example of the Scotswoman may seem quite out of the
ordinary, but in my experience it is the exact opposite—many
psychotherapists work in this way. Their own narcissism is channelled into the therapeutic process, and so the true self of the
patient is not established as the basis of mental health. It is quite
clear that, in the case of the Scot, she had pushed away her natural
self, the self that would have been present had she met the same
man at a party. I have on several occasions taken supervision
groups and asked each person at different times what they felt
when a patient was saying something. In every case, I got replies
not at all dissimilar from the one I received from the Scotswoman.
Note that the second time I asked her what she felt about the man
making derogatory remarks, she again replied: "I felt that he was
trying to say how inferior he was". She said, "I felt" when in fact
that was not how she felt. It was how she thought she *ought* to feel.
When a patient says at the end of a therapy that he feels much
better, it is often a statement of how he thinks he *ought* to feel.
Within a year or so his natural self, his true feeling, surfaces again.
So, once more, he feels depressed and will be in need of help. Next
time, however, he will not have much hope that psychotherapy
will be able to help him.

Narcissistic patients—
the problems for a psychotherapy unit

When Freud was engaged in his researches into the human mind, he believed that it was not possible to treat someone with a narcissistic disorder. This was consistent with his formulation that the narcissistic person has all his libidinal impulses focused on his own self and therefore there are no libidinal strivings stretching out towards the other. Psychoanalytic treatment was based on the idea of transference—libidinal impulses stretching out from the patient towards the analyst. Freud therefore thought, quite logically, that no transference could occur or did occur where someone was suffering some narcissistic disorder.

Subsequent discoveries have shown Freud to be wrong, and wrong from two different angles. The first is that no human being can entirely cut himself off from some emotional attachment to another, even though this attachment may be very much reduced. In fact, we have learned that, in the narcissistic patient, the amount of dependency and attachment is much greater than that in a neurotic patient. The other angle is that, although a narcissistic person puts out libidinal strivings or emotional tentacles, as it were, towards the other only to a limited degree, he is very affected by the actions of another person towards him. This is particularly the case when that other person is someone he idealizes. In the therapeutic situation, therefore, the analyst's or psychotherapist's actions affect the narcissistic patient.

Before I go on, however, I think it would be unwise to dismiss altogether what Freud has said. Although in one sense he was wrong, if we think of his statement as a cautionary tale then he was right. There is no doubt that people with a narcissistic disorder are extremely difficult to treat; with most patients who are narcissistic, the condition itself is not touched. It is my experience that narcissism is the root pathology of nearly all patients who are referred to a psychotherapy unit in a hospital. We now believe that Freud was wrong, since people with narcissistic currents have been treated quite successfully, but it would be extreme omnipotence to believe that treatment is in any way easy. I wish to stress this because I have come across quite a number of psychotherapists who have attended a training course, read some books on the treatment of narcissism, and have set forth with swashbuckling confidence that they are now quite able to treat people with narcissism. I want to emphasize that a narcissistic disorder is something extremely difficult to treat; it is not at all susceptible to easy cure and always involves treatment that is in its nature intensive and lengthy. So, although Freud was wrong—and I do not want to pretend that he was not—we would be wise to weigh his words carefully.

The difficulties of "reading" the patient

How was it that Freud, who was a keen clinical observer, made this factual mistake? His quite logical deduction that narcissistic disorders could not be treated by psychodynamic means was partly to blame. But the main reason was probably because it did not *appear* that narcissistic people were in any affected by the interventions of the analyst. If you do not perceive the way in which a person is affected, then your interpretations will miss the point altogether and have no effect. You can sit back and say to your colleagues: "I treated this patient and made interpretations that I thought were correct—sometimes even the patient assented to the fact that they were correct—and yet the patient did not improve at all." There is in this an implicit blame placed upon the patient. "I did all I could, it was not my fault at all." The truth of the matter is that what the analyst said or did may have had an enormous impact on the narcissistic patient, but the analyst did not notice it. To the trained eye, it is sometimes possible to detect the flicker of an eyelid, a minute change in the tone of voice, or some minuscule bodily reaction. But even if such signals are there, if you do not see them it is as if they do not exist. If the words of the psychotherapist have had an effect, albeit undetected, on the patient, is this effect registered at all in the mind of the patient? The following examples may answer that.

EXTREME REACTIONS

The first example is from my book, *The Analytic Experience* (1986). The example concerns a colleague of mine who had

been treating a woman for about three years in individual psychotherapy on a once-a-week basis, every Monday at 11 a.m.
She was a sophisticated woman. One Monday, my colleague
announced that he had to cancel the session for the following
Monday. His patient nodded, said that it was quite all right,
and gave no outward indication that she was troubled by it.
My colleague, however, did say to her that he thought she was
upset at his having cancelled the session. She replied to him,
with a very superior air, "Do you *really* think that I can't manage without you for just one session, after I have been coming
to see you for three years? Don't you think that your therapy
has had any beneficial effect on me?" My colleague, unwisely,
took her statement at face value. The following week, on the
Monday, at exactly 11 a.m., my colleague's patient took out a
knife and stabbed her boss at work.

* * *

Another example concerns a psychoanalyst in Germany who
was treating a patient who had been in a very disturbed
state—so disturbed that she had been coming to him daily.
However, it appeared that she was a good deal better than she
had been, and between them the analyst and the patient
agreed that it would be all right for her to go and visit some of
her family in Berlin for four days. On the fourth day of her
visit, the patient rang from Berlin and told her analyst that, as
things had gone very well and she felt quite all right, would he
agree to her staying on for a further three days? The analyst
unwisely said that he thought it would be in order. She put
the receiver down, took a knife, and stabbed herself. By a piece
of good fortune, she missed her heart and, although badly
wounded, did not die. When she had completely recovered,
she returned to the analyst. It was then possible to understand
how the innocent words of the analyst had been interpreted:
she had said to herself that his words indicated that he could
not stand her and had therefore asked her to stay away for a
further three days.

* * *

Although these two cases are very extreme, they are in no way
rare. My experience in Australia has not been as extensive in this

field as I would have wished, but, nevertheless, I have supervised a certain number of psychiatric registrars in major hospitals. Not just some, but most, of the patients they are treating are narcissistic or borderline and are just as disturbed as the patients in the examples given. This does not mean that the manifestation of the disturbance is always as dramatic, but I give you two further examples in which the patient was just as disturbed and the reaction in some ways just as serious, though not expressed so dramatically.

RESENTMENT

I was supervising a psychotherapist who was seeing a man who had had a psychotic breakdown two years before and who had now come again for therapy because he felt himself getting very tense and wanted to avert a further breakdown. The psychotherapist was seeing him in a hospital setting twice a week. The psychotherapist was a psychiatric registrar and so had many other duties, as a result of which he was sometimes late—sometimes five minutes, sometimes ten. He would always apologize to the patient, who would say that it was quite all right and he did not mind waiting.

Early on in the treatment, I did not make any comment to the psychotherapist about the situation. The following pattern began to emerge. When the psychotherapist was late, in the subsequent session the patient would invariably start by complaining about his wife, telling the psychotherapist how his wife had been shitty towards him when he arrived home. When the psychotherapist was on time, there was no such occurrence at the following session. It was only after three months of supervision, when the pattern was clear to see and absolutely predictable, that I pointed it out to the psychotherapist. Until I pointed it out, it had never crossed his mind that the times when the patient complained about his wife's shittiness towards him always coincided with the days when he had arrived late. The mechanism was that the patient stored up all his resentment and aimed it at his wife, whereupon she became shitty towards him. It should be pointed out that the patient was quite unaware that he was being in any way disagreeable towards his wife when he arrived home. It was only after the psychotherapist pointed it all out to him that he saw that it was extremely likely that he was offloading the resentment he felt towards the psychotherapist onto his wife.

* * *

I now give you another example, which is not dissimilar. On this occasion, the psychiatric registrar was seeing a patient once a week in his office in the hospital, an office he had to share with another registrar. Four times out of five, he would see the patient in his own room, but, on the fifth occasion, he would have to see him in some other room in the hospital. This man had a drinking problem; every time the psychotherapist had to see him in the other room, that evening he would embark on an alcoholic binge. In this case, again, the patient did not show the slightest sign of being perturbed by anything.

Emotional suppression

My experience is that the majority of patients who are referred for psychotherapy to psychiatric units within public hospitals suffer from a narcissistic disorder or borderline pathology, and patients in these categories are invariably affected in the sorts of ways I have been trying to illustrate. In the type of training most of us receive when we are training to become psychotherapists, we tend to concentrate on what is said to us. The problem with patients of this sort is that they are unable to say what their problems are. If it were possible for a patient to express his emotional state in words, he would not be borderline, would not be suffering from a narcissistic disorder, and would not have been referred in the first place. The disturbance is enacted in interpersonal behaviour outside the consulting-room. Frequently, the patient is most obliging towards the psychotherapist and gives the impression that he is not affected at all by what the psychotherapist has done.

Training the psychotherapist

I believe that the situation among both trainee and qualified psychiatrists is one in which the training given is not equipping him to do the job required of him. It is as if someone has been taught how to drive a car, when actually what is required of him is to pilot a plane. I believe, therefore, that the situation is a serious one: there is nothing to convince me that the patients who are being referred for psychotherapy in hospitals are in any way being cured. Very frequently, the patient will tell the psychotherapist at the end of the therapy that he feels much better; although he may say that, in reality he is no better—he is still offloading all his resentment onto his wife and he is still going on a drunken binge when something upsets him. The truth of whether or not the patient actually is better does not lie in what he says to the psychotherapist but in his actions, particularly emotional activity towards intimates.

I now want to outline what I think are the essential elements for a psychotherapy unit's training which would equip it to deal with the sorts of patient who are being referred. These elements can be dealt with under three different aspects.

1.   The emotional environment of the psychotherapy unit.
2.   An observational style within the psychotherapeutic model.
3.   The consequence of protective actions.

The emotional environment

We are not accustomed to thinking in emotional terms, yet to treat a disturbed patient is an endeavour that requires enormous emotional resources. It is difficult to realize the extent to which thinking has been reserved for comprehension of the inanimate world. Thinking directed to emotional life is in its infancy. A psychoanalyst trained in psychotic processes would observe and monitor a patient in whom these processes are present in situations that would not be given the designation of psychotic in a psychiatric diagnosis. The reason is that the psychiatric designa-

tion of psychosis concerns observed phenomena, such as halluci-
nations, paranoid delusions, and so on. When psychoanalysts use
the word "psychotic", they refer to the inner activity that produces such phenomena but, at the same time, produces other
phenomena. So, for instance, a psychotic mechanism, as understood by a psychoanalyst, can produce hallucination, a paranoid
delusion, a drinking bout, or an irritable wife. The range of phenomena produced by an inner mechanism is much wider than
that set out in a psychiatric textbook. When a psychoanalyst uses
the term "psychotic", he refers to the inner emotional action pattern that produces a range of phenomena.

So, for instance, the first case that I quoted, of the woman who
stabbed her boss, was a manifestation of a psychotic process that
had been present in her all along, as were the other cases I mentioned, like the man who had drinking binges and the man who
offloaded his resentment onto his wife. These occurred because of
the psychotic processes within. I believe that psychiatrists need to
note this wide array of phenomena and perhaps find a term with
which to describe them.

There was a time when trainee psychotherapists were given
patients with just mild neuroses—it was reckoned that such patients were the best sort of training material. Even if this were
desirable, it is just not the case today, because the patients who are
referred always have areas of psychotic functioning. Again, I need
to stress that I am using this term in the psychoanalytic sense: that
there are inner action patterns that are operating against the inner
apparatus that apprehends reality. So the problem needs to be
faced squarely and addressed appropriately. The first thing that is
necessary is that psychotherapists, when taking on a patient of
this kind, need great emotional support. Psychotherapy units
must have a firm goal clearly stated. What also needs to be considered are the requirements necessary for the unit to fulfil its joint
tasks—both of successfully treating narcissistic patients and those
with a borderline pathology that derives from narcissism, and of
giving psychiatric registrars adequate training in the treatment of
these patients.

It is a fact that trainee psychiatrists model themselves on the
behaviour and attitudes of their superiors. Therefore, the director

or directors of a psychotherapy unit need to demonstrate by their own personal behaviour that the people within their domain are cared for. They need to demonstrate through their own personal conduct what their priorities are. They will therefore ensure that the timetable, once it has been worked out, is kept to and that only in exceptional circumstances will they allow timetables to be altered. But the most important thing, apart from supervision, is that the psychiatrist who is treating narcissistic patients can rely upon emotional support. I cannot emphasize too much the emotional stress that these patients put upon the treating psychiatrist, the psychiatrist who is treating them with psychotherapy. The structure needs to be such that not only is the patient held in a secure framework by the psychotherapist, but the psychotherapist himself is also held within a firm framework. This framework, made up out of a group of staff, should make him feel secure. You may say that such a structure patronizes or infantilizes the psychotherapist.

In the First World War, when a lot of ships were being sunk by the Germans, Lloyd George proposed that merchant ships be surrounded by battle cruisers and other ships that would form a protective cordon around them while under sail, often with valuable cargoes. The naval commanders laughed at Lloyd George's proposal, saying that he was treating them as if the individual ship commanders and ships were babies in a nursery. Luckily, this taunt did not deter Lloyd George, who gave orders for his plan to be put into effect. So originated what became known as the convoy, and it saved millions of tonnes of shipping from going to the bottom of the sea during the First World War.

Psychotherapists treating disturbed patients also need a protective convoy, and this means that both the time and the space necessary to facilitate such a structure have to be carved out. I am more than aware that the pressures against this are often enormous, but this is a battle that needs to be won. It is also a source of great confidence to the psychotherapist when he knows that the director of the unit has made his work both possible and free from interruption.

In addition to individual supervision, those who are treating the narcissistic patient need the support of the group. I do not mean anything wishy-washy when I use the word "support". I mean that the individual should feel able to reveal his difficulties with the patient in a setting in which he feels he can receive help, support, understanding, and criticism of a constructive nature from those who are in the same boat as himself. The necessity for this weekly meeting cannot be over-emphasized. I have been referring to trainees, but qualified psychiatrists treating these patients need such a group as well. I believe that it is not possible for any individual to treat these patients without a support structure of this nature.

Churchill said in one of his early speeches during the Second World War that the Allies would feel a closer bond between themselves after the War for having "walked through the fire together". Psychotherapists who experience the bond of "walking through the fire together" will be in an incomparably better position to treat these patients than those who are doing it in an isolated way and with little sense of support. The problems that these patients present are not cured through the arrival of a new theory, a new piece of technique, or a special kind of interpretation, but rather through the emotional ability of the psychotherapist to withstand the stress that such patients place upon them. I am conscious that I am going on about this, but I do so because I see little evidence that the emotional problems that these patients present have been in any way appreciated.

The observational style

I want to turn now to the second attitude of mind that is essential for the successful treatment of these patients. It is that the psychotherapist needs to think of the endeavour that he is engaged in as an observational procedure. I do not mean by this that he needs to stay detached. The psychotherapist cannot stay detached, even if he wishes it. Patients with psychotic processes draw in the psychotherapist whether he wants to be drawn in or not, whether he believes that this is happening or not. When the patient acts out because the psychotherapist is absent, that psychotherapist cannot say he is not involved. He may prefer not to be involved, he may say that he wishes he had never taken on this patient, but the truth of the matter is that he did. The psychotherapist's attitude of mind should be one of observation; in particular, observation of changes in emotional moods and attitudes.

It is very unlikely that a psychotherapist, in the early stages, or even in the later stages, will be able to understand why this kind of behaviour is occurring. It is a very great achievement if the psychotherapist is able to observe the psychotic behaviour at all. For instance, in the case of the man who unloaded his resentment onto his wife whenever the psychotherapist was five or ten minutes late for a session, it was a big achievement to observe the connection between these two events, for it was then possible to name it and for the patient to be able to see it. Once something like this has been seen, then given patience and tolerance the meaning of the observed behaviour will emerge. If the psychotherapist is not too anxious, does not feel that he has to quickly apply a plaster made up of a piece of theory or a quickly summed-up interpretation, the meaning will emerge. I believe that this attitude of observation is possible only if the psychotherapist has the support of his colleagues in the way described. Just one observation of this sort in the course of a therapy—say, a piece of therapy lasting two years—is worth a whole rash of interpretations based upon a theory or group of theories.

It also has other advantages that are extremely significant. In such a situation, the patient feels that he is participating in the process of understanding, helping to build an understanding. This is one aspect of it. The other aspect is that the psychotherapist is able to bring back these observations to the group, so the group slowly begins to accumulate a body of observed knowledge that makes sense. The psychotherapy unit begins to have a culture of its own, with its own understanding.

I know that what I am suggesting flies in the face of those who would recommend a supportive psychotherapy with a more active direction for borderline patients. There may be some reading this who prefer such an approach.

Relating to the patient's emotional mechanisms

The third of the principles that I have outlined is the ability to recognize that the patient is partially responsible for the suffering and distress that brings him for treatment. In the earlier part of this century, most patients who came for psychotherapy had some quite clearly identifiable emotional disorder, thought to originate in some emotional difficulty: hysterical conversion, obsessional symptomatology, manic-depressive psychosis, schizophrenia, schizoid conditions, or a psychic condition such as depression. Many patients today present themselves in distress arising from a series of failed relationships. The failure of the relationships frequently originates in some psychotic process, and therefore very often these patients are referred to as borderline or narcissistic. These failed relationships are just another manifestation of the psychotic processes that produced the more classical conditions that seemed to be more common earlier in this century or in less-developed cultures. Many patients come for assessment with an account of emotional exploitation, and, although their problems are attributed to external causes, there is a covert knowledge that they are partly a consequence of things that happen within. In other words, the patients are doing something that brings these disasters on themselves.

I say this because his training does not currently equip the psychotherapist for the sort of problems that he meets, although a great deal of it concentrates upon the failures, the lack of good loving, and so on that have befallen the patient. A general style of psychotherapy arises that sees the patient as a victim of traumatic events. Of course, we are all moulded by the things that have happened to us in our childhood, but it is crucial for the psychotherapist to investigate what the inner emotional response of the patient has been and what the continuing response is. In other words, what is the patient unwittingly doing that gets him into such trouble? I am here talking about very subtle emotional activities of which the patient is quite unaware. Very often these activities are part of the patient's ways of coping with some traumatic event from childhood, but what the psychotherapist has to address are the emotional mechanisms existing in the present. A good example is the case of erotic transference I quoted in chapter seven of the young woman, Sophia, in London, whose new boyfriend, Michael, became impotent, as all her other lovers had done. That case illustrates quite well the level of the emotional action that I am referring to—the young woman was bringing the situation upon her own head through an activity of which she was not aware. The psychotherapist needs to be able to connect at this level of emotional activity in order to help patients to reverse and change the responses of people to them and so restructure the social contours of their lives. When we say that sensitivity is necessary in a psychotherapist, it is not just sensitivity to this level of emotional functioning that is required, but also emotional strength. My experience is that most of us are not aware of the effect that we have upon our patients. I have mentioned cases in which patients were affected by the room in which they were treated, the psychotherapist's punctuality or reliability, and other such elements of the outer structure of the treatment. This last case, where I finally managed to articulate an interpretation, serves to emphasize more subtle emotional factors that have just as powerful an effect upon the patient. We need extreme sensitivity combined with great emotional strength, and we cannot do it without being flanked by the support of colleagues.

Conclusion

I want to end by saying that narcissism always crushes individual creative emotional action: it converts it from being constructive to being destructive. There are, of course, many creative people who are narcissistic. However, I believe that their narcissism interferes with creativity, as their creative capacities have grown as their narcissism has lessened. The task of a psychotherapist is to start the process of transforming narcissism and to change what is destructive to a constructive emotional action. I believe that this goal can be achieved if the training of a psychotherapy unit is focused on the three elements discussed above. These are that the unit must provide a supportive environment; the psychotherapist must maintain an attitude of observation; and the psychotherapist must also have a firm realization that the patient's subtle emotional level contributes to his unfortunate situation, especially where intimate relationships are involved. If training is so focused, I believe our chances of improving our results with narcissistic patients will be greatly enhanced.

CHAPTER TWELVE

An analysis of greed

L ooking harassed, Mummy bustled into the kitchen. The three children were lolling around waiting for her. It was tea-time.

She opened the biscuit tin. "Heavens," she cried, "where have they all gone?" and looked accusingly at Tom, Mary, and Jane. Tom rushed over, looked in, and exclaimed, "There are heaps there still". "It was full when I left. Where have they all gone, where have they all gone?", his mother wailed.

Greed inhibiting the therapeutic process

For four years, I had been conducting the analysis of a woman I shall call Mary. She was a left-wing sociologist living in Brixton, a suburb of London south of the Thames, and she came to see me in Hampstead.

She was very poor and had scraped together the fees to see me by approaching a variety of people she knew who had done very well in their professions. Mary hated the fact that they (and this included me) were capable of earning their own living, whereas she was not. In this, I saw the dragon of envy and made interpretations about it, but they had no substantial effect. Her life structure *did* improve, however, and she reached a stage where she could pay my fees out of her earnings. She asserted herself more and allowed herself to be exploited less. She got a couple of lectureships, the responsibilities of which she handled extremely well, although she went through an inner torture over the delivery of the lectures. Her emotional life, however, was empty.

In the early phases of the analysis, I enjoyed seeing her. Mary had a quick mind, understood things, and seemed fond of me. She found breaks very difficult. There was a tendency in her to want to turn a session into an intellectual discussion, and it took some time to educate her into the emotional work of the analysis. She grasped things easily, sessions seemed to go well, and she felt that her view of the world had been radically altered through being in analysis. She used analytical insight for her work as a sociologist but felt guilty about it. I made interpretations about a feeling that she was getting inside me and robbing me of my goods, and she agreed I was right. She very rarely disagreed, and on several occasions said that I had always been right on certain issues, and this led her to trust me.

This all sounded very good indeed. There was only one thing wrong—her emotional life did not change one iota. I was reminded of that cautionary limerick for drivers of cars:

> Here lies the body of Liza Grey
> Who died asserting her right of way
> She was right, dead right, as she sped along
> But she's still as dead as if she'd been wrong.

I began to feel a bit like Mummy, whom I had introduced at the beginning, and wanted to ask, "Where have all my interpretations gone?"

Then, one day, I caught the culprit red-handed. Luckily, she gave herself up and came along to the police station without a struggle. Mary was talking about Sally: Sally had led her to realize that her last series of lectures had not been very good; Sally always brought her down to earth and made her face reality. She went on to say that she had been wondering whether to carry on as a lecturer. When she said this, I knew certain things. I knew Sally had been let in as an underminer. To carry on as a lecturer was the equivalent of persevering with the analysis. I knew that something had happened, and whatever it was had made her give up and let Sally in. As confirmation, her tone was desultory, and her words did not ring true.

"Ah, yes!", I said to myself. "When she arrived and crossed the hall into the waiting room, she had seen me going out of the consulting-room into the house with an empty mug." (My wife and I both practised from home when we lived and worked in London.) So I said to her, "When you arrived, you saw me go into the house with a coffee mug. At that moment, you caught a glimpse of me and that woman together in the house. You then sighed and gave up and said, 'I am not going to persevere any longer with this analysis. I'll invite Sally in; at least she'll be faithful to me, unlike this analyst who has now betrayed me'."

Suddenly she screamed, "How do you do it? How do you do it? I was talking about something completely different and you alight on it. You are right, but I can't bear not knowing how you do it."

I replied, "You have now grabbed the interpretation. You are so desperate to learn the secret of how the golden egg is laid that you grab it. This time, it was right and you grabbed it, but you grab it whether it is right or wrong. Good interpretations and bad ones all get stuffed in. Your eyes are bigger than your belly. You are watching with those eyes, all the time, as each interpretation comes out. Then you grab it, but because you grab it, stuff it inside you without chewing and digesting it, you guiltily shit it out again in a lecture. The problem is that you are so fixated on how I am doing it and grabbing it before that woman in the house gets it, that you do not listen to interpretations. Listening means considering whether it is good for you or not. You do not take it in. You grabbed this interpretation and numerous others over the last two years. This is why you are stuck—the same old rows with your boyfriend each week, and not an iota of progress."

Here was this pleasant woman understanding all my interpretations—except that, in an essential area of her life, I knew and she knew that we were not getting anywhere. Until that moment, I did not know why, but I did know that the interpretations were not going in. In fact, that is not correct—they were being grabbed and stuffed in indiscriminately. This grabbing was at a subtle level. Greed was constituted in this grabbing—no space given for consideration. I was only aware of the effects of it: that the tin of interpretations had all gone.

I think you have all had the experience of sitting at a table with a child. Someone brings a plate of biscuits, and the child grabs one of them. You feel robbed, not because the biscuit has been taken, but because it has been grabbed. Greed lies not in the taking but in the manner of the taking. The object, the breast, is taken in, but it is taken in very differently from an experience that is nurturing.

I want now to examine the quality of this taking in that we call greed. I believe that if we can see the elements in it, then it will help us to recognize it when we encounter it in the transference.

The well-hidden sin

It is important we *know* about greed because it is so hidden. Mary was a nice woman and I had not *seen* a hint of greed, but had I known the essential elements of the greedy relationship to the breast, I believe that I should have focused in on the essentials much more quickly. (I want here to caution against the attitude that in analysis we have a long time and that we can afford to wait, that we have years in front of us. In analysis, we have a big job to do and we have no time to waste. If we waste time, psycho-analysis becomes an indulgence.)

I had spoken to Mary a great deal about greed. I had used the image of a piranha fish, which she had understood and assented to, but her relations to me in the transference, which were dominated by this greedy part of her, had not been managed. Her feelings were not engaged in the matter. We had also spoken often about a Miss Prim, who brushed away all the shitty unpleasant parts of herself. She had a very idealized image of herself. Capitalists, especially analysts, were greedy, but she was dedicated to the underdog. This, however, does not give a fair picture of her. She had a kind, outgoing nature, loved animals, and easily became tearful. You would say she was affectionate. She was thoughtful towards others and went out of her way to be helpful to people. So when she and I talked of greed together, it was her kind, co-operative side that was trying to be helpful to me. That there was a greedy devouring side was undoubtedly true. It took time to see the way she was devouring my interpretations for her sociological use. It became clearer why she wanted to keep everything at an intellectual level. She could not bear the image of herself as a greedy piranha fish, which was so at odds with the Miss Prim image of herself. That she protected herself from the full force of feeling in the analysis, I was certain.

I had an intellectual conviction that she did not want me to penetrate through to this greedy part of her. I say all this in order to introduce you to an error I made when the greedy split-off part came into the transference relationship. I went on relentlessly interpreting this split-off part, and she began to feel that there were two of her at such a disjunction from each other. I put so much weight on this split-off part that the malevolent shadow devoured the good and the analysis came to an end. I saw in front of my eyes the explosion that can occur when two opposites crash into one another. What occurred is exactly as Bion (1953, p. 33) has described.

I say all this as a kind of warning. If I had this patient again, I would interpret the powerful greed but, at the same time, the powerful desire for integration. At such a point, the analyst needs, I believe, to act as mediator so that powerful contrary forces can be brought into conjunction with one another. The niceness in Mary needed something of the force of that greedy person in her, just as that greedy person needed something of the gentle affection.

The elements of greed

Greed, I believe, is hidden under shame, so when it comes to light it is a crisis for the individual. Its elements are cleverly hidden because the individual is ashamed of them. We need to know what the elements of greed are so that we can recognize the signs, which may very easily escape us unless we are on the look-out. Sherlock Holmes attended not to the obvious but to small signs, which Dr Watson unfailingly missed. We, however, must start with the obvious and try to work things out from there.

The envious look bores into the other person, into the object. The greedy look grabs what the other is giving. When someone comes for psychoanalysis, I want to *give* to the patient: I want to give what *I* understand, not what my supervisor has told me, not what Melanie Klein or Winnicott have told me, not what my own analyst told me, but what *I* understand. My understanding has been wrested from the struggles of the heart throughout my life. It is *that* that the analyst is prepared to give when he takes a patient into psychoanalysis. It is extremely difficult to give something that is so precious and has been so hard-won in the face of someone who grabs it and stuffs it in and churns it up with a whole lot of junk food. In subtle ways, the analyst curbs his generosity. Here, then, is the first principle: greed stops the other giving; so, in therapy, the patient stops the analyst giving. The greed, however, never encompasses the whole personality but is only a part of it, with its origins in the part-object phase of development. I need to give some explanation of this.

Mythology that personifies the vices and virtues has seized on an essential psychological truth. Greed is not a drive or an instinct, but functions as a person within the personality. When the analyst finds his generosity curbed, he is witnessing an inner drama in which his generous impulses are seized by greed. The ultimate effect is to seal off emotional contact between the analyst and the patient, and to seal off contact between one part of the self and another. Greed keeps the personality system sealed off from cross-fertilization with the social world around.

As a boy, I was going off one day on a train back to school. An elderly woman, a friend of the family, gave me some sweets but instructed me to keep them and eat them myself, and not to offer them to the other children. This is the function of greed in the personality: keep the goods in yourself and do not share. I had a patient once whose analysis spread out from him, and his wife and children began to experience the benefit of it. At a certain point, however, greed stepped in and strangled what was happening. The analysis went into the doldrums, and I felt dispirited. Greed will not let the analysis cross the boundaries of inner space and incorporate the outer. This was the case with Mary—the analysis seemed to be working very well between us, but there it remained. Greed stopped it spreading out to incorporate within it the people or potential people in her life. So here is another principle: greed keeps the analysis confined to inner space and stops it crossing over to include the important others of the person's social world.

I agree with Melanie Klein (1957, p. 181) that greed and envy are closely intertwined and that the one does not exist without the other. Although the greedy baby is a well-recognized phenomenon that we encounter regularly in the consulting-room, analysts have focused much more upon envy. Envy, however, is different from greed. While the envious person expels the bad aspects of himself into the envied object, the greedy person snatches the good in the other. I have said that what is taken from the other is not digested, so what is done with it? It is, in fact, not truly taken in: it is taken but not digested. What is the relation, then, to a stolen but undigested object? In ordinary life, the individual hides the stolen goods; in the psychological process, the thief hides his own person in the very object he has stolen. He becomes the guilty possessor of his stolen object. The person who eats and drinks greedily also becomes the victim of his own greed through a hangover or a liver attack. What is the exact nature of this psychological "grab" that turns nurture for the mind into a reverse process in which the mind becomes the slave of its own servant?

The individual in the grip of greed *watches* the outer object, dazzled by its brightness. The personality is focused on the productions of the outer object and is divorced from his own inner emotional requirements. Possessed by greed, he is cut off from what he requires, cut off from who he inwardly is. Personal relations dominated by greed are those whose focus is on the outer manifestation. Greed causes the eye of the mind to turn outwards and defies psychoanalysis, the aim of which is to turn the eye of the mind inwards. Greed is the implacable enemy of its purposes.

When an interpretation is taken in without greed, the patient has no need to hide it—he feels all right about it. It is done with respect towards the analyst and with his knowledge. Another sign, then, of greed is that the interpretation is taken silently, secretly, and without acknowledgement.

The obliterator of persons

However, we are still wrestling to understand the form of the psychological act that makes greed what it is. To answer this, I want to state a principle: it is not psychologically possible for Greed to grab from another unless it has an ally. Therefore, Greed has an ally without whom he cannot do his work. This ally destroys the personhood of the other, who may be the analyst, the mother, the brother, the wife, or the husband and can be called the Obliterator of Persons. It is inherent in the nature of personal relations that the Obliterator cancels out the personhood of both participants of the relationship. Therefore, the personhood of the analyst and the patient are obliterated. This is not, itself, Greed's activity, but he cannot do it without this ally. The most common manifestation of this in the transference is idealization. In the presence of Greed, the tackling of this idealization is the central focus of the analysis from the very beginning. I had intimated that this greed is laid down from a very early phase of development, and therefore daily work has to be done on it. Where Greed has a powerful grip on the psychological functioning of the personality,

I think it naive to imagine that an analyst will begin to see any lessening of its power in less than four years. And then at four years one might see a beginning, and then a lot of work will be needed to bring that first beginning to full bloom. It will be hard daily work with many setbacks, but nothing less than this will have any effect. I believe that more superficial therapies, even those based on psychoanalytic principles, make no inroads upon this deep-rooted moral deformity that controls events at the core of the personality.

Therefore, when greed dominates the structure of intimacy, it vitiates personal relationships through the action of the ally, the Obliterator. It also means that relationships are shorn of fruitfulness, so that no change can take place. A relationship between two people, each perceived as a whole object, demands change in each in order for a relationship to occur. A yielding of self-oriented libido has to occur. Greed, then, is generated through a deep-seated narcissistic orientation and kept in being through it. It cannot be tackled on its own—it has to be tackled along with the narcissistic choice in which it is embedded along with its allies, the Obliterator, Envy, Meanness, and Omnipotence. It is always surrounded by these other guardians of the fortress. I do not want to discuss the interrelations between them here, except to point out that all these have to be tackled if Greed's stranglehold on the personality is to be lessened. I want, however, to distinguish Greed from Envy, so that it can be recognized when it emerges in the clinical situation.

Conclusion

In an exchange between two persons, there is also an exchange of gifts. The analyst is someone who gives freely of his insight about the other. What does the patient give to the analyst? Quite simply, he gives himself. When Greed is dominant, the patient takes but does not give, and it is this taking in the absence of psychological giving that constitutes Greed. It is through reflection, over time, that this silent Greed can be recognized, and it is the analyst's job to help the patient towards this recognition. It is not easy, but if the analyst does it, it will bring enrichment into the patient's life. Quite simply, it can transform relationships governed by concu-piscence into friendship. If an analyst can do that for his patient, then he has really done something. I am unable to imagine a greater transfor-mation or one that is more worthwhile.

I cannot end without sharing with you this vignette:

When I was just qualified as an analyst, I was treating a very deprived adolescent in a clinic in London. I was presenting him to three of my colleagues, and one of them said to me, "You need to interpret his greed". I protested that the boy was deprived and forlorn. Someone else at the meeting then told of a child psychotherapist working in Bombay with starving children. He said to me, "The psychotherapist did not get anywhere with these children until she began to interpret their greed". That was many years ago, but it made a lasting impression on me.

CHAPTER THIRTEEN

The origins
of rage and aggression

It is a mistake to think that psychoanalysis has one theory. Psychoanalysis is a clinical methodology that encompasses a wide range of theories, and nowhere is this more evident than when psychoanalysts start to discuss the cause of aggression. At its most simple, there are two theories.

The first states that aggression arises when a human being's basic needs are frustrated. This theory is based upon the homeostatic theory of motivation, which states that the organism has a built-in tendency to equilibrium, to homeostasis—that when inner tension arises, the organism is programmed to reduce that tension through incorporating food or water or finding an object that will satisfy a sexual need. Aggression arises when one of these needs is frustrated; aggression is therefore a reaction to frustration. The second theory states that aggression is a basic instinct in man. In summary, then, those who support the second theory say that man is a savage creature by nature, whereas those who support the first theory believe that man is essentially benign and only becomes savage when frustrated of his basic biological needs. I believe that both theories are wrong.

The homeostatic theory is wrong because it fails to account adequately for certain areas of human experience, like a person's love of beauty, the individual who dies for his country, and certain emotional and mental satisfactions in pursuit of which an individual will be prepared to sacrifice pleasures associated with the homeostatic theory. Although there must be few analysts today who hold the homeostatic theory, many believe what is in fact one of its consequences: that aggression arises through frustration of a basic biological need. Some would extend this to include frustration of emotional needs. The theory that man is innately aggressive does not give sufficient account of the transformations of instinct that have progressively taken place in the evolution of mankind. I want therefore to put forward another theory. To do this, I start from an experience and its interpretation.

An appalling crime

In the early 1970s, I worked as a psychotherapist at Grendon Prison near Aylesbury in England. Grendon is a psychiatric prison, and group therapy was the treatment of choice. Some of you may have read the book on Grendon Prison, *The Frying Pan* (1970), by Tony Parker. I was associated at this time with an organization whose goal was the social rehabilitation of prisoners and whose philosophy was that rehabilitation started from the day a man first went to prison.

To pursue this philosophy, I went one day to interview a man who had just been remanded in custody at Wandsworth Prison. This young man had entered the house next door to where he lived and found there a 10-year-old girl, Isabella. He pulled her by the hair around the top landing and then dragged her screaming down the stairs. When he got her to the ground floor, he raped her and then killed her by bashing her head against a wall.

I was shown by the warder into the interview room, where I sat on a wooden upright chair with the prisoner opposite me and a bare wooden table between us. The prisoner spoke in an affectionate manner towards me, although nervous. He looked very young; I cannot remember his age, but he did not look over 21. He seemed bewildered, as if he had been catapulted into this world from another planet. After explaining to him the purpose of my visit and asking him for the date of his trial, he gave me some details about his legal representation. I then set about asking him about the crime. He had known Isabella quite well, I gathered. On the day of the crime, he had gone to the greengrocers on his bicycle. When he had returned, he had seen Isabella in the garden and had gone to play with her. Then there had been an accident. I pressed him to tell me exactly what had happened.

"We were playing along the stairs; she screamed."

"What made her scream?"

"She was hurt."

"Can you remember what happened?"

"It wouldn't have happened if her mother had been there. She should have come back. Young children should not be left on their own. You never know what might happen to them."

He then wandered off as if in a dream. He started to talk of Isabella's mother, Josephine. "We used to be together, you see."

"You mean you were having an affair?"

He smiled with embarrassment and guilt. I pressed him to talk, but he remained silent, so I turned to talking of other things. Then he murmured, "Isabella saw us".

"Is that what made you attack her?"

"Hair. Oh heavens . . . stairs."

He then murmured, "Accident . . . Oh no!" He was now only semi-talking to me. I had the impression that some visual images were flashing across the memory screen and he was reacting to them. At this point in the conversation, a very strange thing happened to me. I fell asleep, or at least I would have done had I not struggled with all my might against it. It was in the morning and I was sitting on a hard, wooden, upright chair. He commented, "What, sleepy?", and he smiled again with embarrassment. It was as if an anaesthetic slug had been fired into me. I struggled on to the end of the interview, but all my energy was directed towards keeping awake. About a week later, I returned for a second interview and, again, when we talked of the crime, he went into his "memory screen" mode and I was overcome with sleepiness. A week after the second interview, he went on trial at the Old Bailey and was found guilty and sentenced to twenty-five years in prison. One morning, a few days later, a prison warder opened up his cell and found he had hanged himself.

The mental state of the accused

I will give you my reconstruction of these events. It was an incontrovertible fact that he had committed the crime of which he was accused. When I was interviewing him, I do not think that he was consciously suppressing knowledge or lying to me. I think a part of his mind had blanked out what had happened so that just the odd flashes came back to him, but not what he had actually done. Some of you may have seen the film *The Boston Strangler* some years ago. After the police had caught him, the film showed a scene in which the psychiatrist was questioning him in interview after interview. After a time, momentary flashes came back to him, as was the case with the man I interviewed. My conjecture is that, subsequent to the trial, memory of what he had done came back to him and he hanged himself.

In a psychoanalytic treatment, the analyst represents a part of the patient's mind which I have termed the *embryo mind*. Speaking generally, we know the mind's enormous potential. The human race has been blessed with Plato, Michelangelo, Shakespeare, Mozart, Kant, Karl Marx, Einstein, and hosts of others too numerous to name. We all know the heights of which the mind is capable. It is my experience as a psychoanalyst that many minds have a latent potential capable of considerable creative emotional work. This is the emotional correlate of what Vygotsky (1934) named the *proximal zone*, by which he meant that part of the mind capable of further cognitive development. The embryo mind is the proximal zone but applied to the emotional sphere of the mind. It is the embryo mind that the analyst represents. The phenomenon of the analyst as external representation of this inner capacity of mind is called the transference.

My mind was knocked for six when I was interviewing this prisoner. On the basis of transference, it leads me to infer that his embryo mind was being violently smothered by a part of the mind that is known in psychoanalytic discourse as the *archaic superego*. I have found a model of the mind in which different parts are, in relation to other parts of the mind, indispensable for understanding the emotional phenomena I encounter in clinical work. So my sensation of being slugged by an anaesthetic dart in itself leads to the inference that his embryo mind was being violently attacked. The fact that the memory of what he had done to Isabella had been almost entirely obliterated confirms such an inference. This paralleled the fact that my mind was not completely knocked out—a small part remained struggling.

Let us look now at the triple constellation that we have here. The first point is that a savage tyrant part of the mind (the archaic superego) is attacking the part of the mind with all the creative potential (the embryo mind), with the result that events of great importance are wiped out. Secondly, the young man attacks a 10-year-old girl with great brutality, and, thirdly, in an interview with the young man, an analyst's mind is nearly knocked unconscious.

The second point is an infamous public event, and the third is a personal private event passing between two people. The first point, however, is an entirely private inner drama.

The unbearable guilt

I now want to trace things in a particular manner and hope that this hypothesis will carry some conviction for you. The prisoner blotted out the memory of what he had done because he was so appallingly guilty. As you can imagine, it was a crime that was reported in all the media and sent ripples of shocked outrage through the community. The world at large experienced the horror that the criminal himself could not experience. It is a phenomenon often observed in clinical psychoanalysis that what is not experienced by the agent himself is projected outwards and experienced in the wider community; so, in this case, the only person who had no conscious horror of the event was the man who had perpetrated it. I contend that to allow himself to know what he had done caused insupportable guilt in the prisoner, and it was this guilt that led him to blot out the memory of his crime. If my conclusion—that the anaesthetizing of my mind was the external correlate of this blotting out of the memory of his crime—is correct, then the source of the attack on my mind was the very same guilt. I now want to take one further step, one that you may be unwilling to take, and that is to say that the emotional origin of that savage attack upon Isabella was also guilt.

Guilt is a feeling consequent upon an action: it makes sense only if the person who did the deed that produced the guilt could have chosen *not* to do the deed. What I am saying, then, is that in the prisoner there was a guilt that led to the killing of Isabella; that there was enormous guilt about the slaughter going on in his mind. When he killed Isabella, he had entirely surrendered himself into the power of that part of his mind which Melanie Klein first named the archaic superego. The guilt over the inner situation was so great that it impelled him to dramatize it in the outer world. When the prisoner's inner drama was catapulted into the outer world, he was put in prison. Punishment is society's revenge against the perpetrator of a crime, but it is also the medicine of healing, and, paradoxically, I believe that to have been the driving motive behind the crime. This concept is illustrated most clearly in Dostoevsky's *Crime and Punishment*. The novel opens with Raskolnikov brutally axing the old woman to death. The main portion of the book describes Raskolnikov's dilemma over whether or not to confess. He finally does confess and is sent off to hard labour in Siberia. The reader understands, however, that through the relationship with Sonia, the punishment is the first step towards recovering a sane mind. With my prisoner, at the moment when recovery might have started, he killed himself.

Conclusion

I believe that guilt is the instigator of violent outbursts of the sort I have tried to describe. In such outbursts, aggression, which is a natural endowment of human beings, is used destructively rather than constructively. I have tried to sketch the activity in the mind that produces this guilt: to go into how these activities in the mind originated would take us into another area of inquiry altogether. What I am stating is that it is guilt—a guilt that is not conscious—that accounts for sudden outbursts of violent rage.

To return to where I started, violent outbursts of murderous rage do not occur because of a biological need becoming frustrated or because aggression is innate in man. The problem lies in whose service the aggression is being employed—it is when it is employed against the potential capacities of the mind that guilt arises. A person does not feel guilt unless there was an alternative activity open to him. The origin of violence lies in guilt. This means that an inner decision has been taken. That the origin of violence is to be found in the ego rather than in an instinctual urge means that it is a personal construction in which it is possible to find meaning. In this there is some hope, because the possibility of constructing things differently is always there. The more we understand guilt and the way it comes about in the mind, the more chance we have of arriving at measures that are prophylactic against the eruption of violence in our society. It is to this that I believe we should address ourselves.

CHAPTER FOURTEEN

The autonomy of the self

T his chapter is based on two papers written in response to Brian Muir's "The Enigma of the Self" (1993), which is a critique of Kohut. I have expanded various points that Brian made and taken them forward in my own way, so hopefully the reader need not have read his original paper to understand my arguments.

It is possible for me to be so engrossed in myself that another person is only perceived to the extent to which he impinges upon me. With such an orientation of mind, I shall try very hard to avoid any such impingements. However, there are a lot of human beings around, and, try as I might, it is difficult to avoid them. As Fairbairn pointed out, I find—much to my annoyance—that there is something in me that drives me towards human beings.

> When I was a baby I was driven, *faute de mieux*, towards a breast. It was an unwelcome discovery when two eyes appeared behind that breast. "What", I cried and bawled. "That breast is mine, it belongs to me, it has no right to attach itself to those two eyes." So I put in a complaint to the Babies' Rights Commission.

When infancy was over, I sighed with relief and said: "Thank God, I can get my own food now". I then entered a wonderful period where I was able to banish all those annoying objects that kept interfering with the pleasant fulfilment of my dreams. All was bliss until suddenly that wretched breast appeared again. I found myself driven to it, and to the eyes as well, which was even more annoying. I returned to my child's logic and said: "If I need them, they must belong to me." Just when I believed firmly that they were mine, the breast, eyes, hair, and voice all detached themselves and took flight, not on a horse but on two mobiles that were at the service of all the rest, called "legs" (or so I was later told). This time I put in a complaint to the Equal Opportunities Board.

I could not rid myself of these unjustified impingements, which had been with me since childhood. It was not fair: after all, I had not asked to be born. Yes, that's a thought, who gave them permission? God, they never even asked me. It's outrageous, so I put in a complaint to the Citizen's Rights Commission, explaining my grievance. Finally, I received this curt reply:

> "We have received your complaint, and, while recognizing the justice of your position, we have, after much deliberation, decided that we cannot take it up on your behalf as it is outside our jurisdiction. We have therefore passed it on to the Demographic and Reproductive Planning Commission."

Five weeks later I received this note from the DRPC:

> While this Commission does everything in its power to limit population to the requirements of this country supplied to it by the Future Planning Commission, it is unable to obtain the consent of the unborn. Although we fully realize the desirability of obtaining such consent, our Scientific Sub-committee has not been able to devise a means whereby this can be achieved, but hopes to do so at some future date.
>
> The members of this Commission were very sympathetic to your complaint and wondered whether you had considered engaging the services of a psychotherapist. We are in touch with the Kohut Association of Psychotherapy which, we are told, is in empathic relation to persons with com-

plaints such as yours. We recommend that you get in touch with this association as we believe that it may be able to resolve your complaint.

We remain, yours faithfully,

For the first time in my life my complaints were sympathetically heard. My psychotherapist, Mr M Pathy, was considerate enough to record my interview with him. He later gave me a copy, which I often play to myself as I find it such a comfort. I know that you will share in my own enjoyment because, if I get comfort from it, then you must too. That is one very wise piece of philosophy that I have learned from Mr M Pathy: anything that is true for me has to be true of all people who enter my orbit. The following is a piece of that first, wonderful conversation:

"I do hope that you are going to listen to my problem, because no one ever does."

"Perhaps people did not listen to you in your childhood?

"No, you're right. My mother was always nagging at me, telling me to brush my teeth after meals, to tie up my shoe-laces and wash my hands before meals."

"And your father?"

"No, he was the same, always backing up my mother, and he always paid more attention to Maria, my sister."

"And this has gone on like this right until now?"

"Yes, my wife nags at me all the time, expecting me to take the children out after I have come home from a hard day's work."

"So no one thinks of you as a person with your own needs?"

"At the weekend, she expects me to help in the garden and clean the house. She never thinks that I have been working all during the week and need a rest at the weekend."

"So no one ever thinks of you?"

"No, they just carry on as if I was the general dogsbody."

"So you feel unappreciated and unloved, perhaps?"

"Yes, I've never felt loved. They're all too concerned with themselves."

"Perhaps you felt unloved by me when I had to cancel last week's session?"

"Oh, no. I did not think that at all. I knew you had an important reason. That's quite different from the way it is at home."

"You mean at home you do not feel cared for?"

"No, not at all, and that's the way it always was when I was a child. No one cared about me. I just always had to be a slave to everyone else."

"No space given for your own personal growth."

[At this point, there is a pause on the tape.]

"So that's why you came here—to have a space for your own personal growth."

"Yes, I've never had that before. People always want things from me."

"It's so unfair."

I'll turn off the tape now, but you can see how comforted I was. I would walk away from Mr M Pathy's consulting-room and drive home and all seemed so wonderful. At last I had found an understanding person, and I felt enwrapped in a soft soothing light. But when I got home, it made the contrast worse: my wife's nagging now seemed intolerable, whereas before it had just been a dull background noise.

On my way to and from Mr M Pathy's consulting-room, I would pass the offices of Mr E Fective, Psychotherapist. The sound of his name caught my attention, for some reason. Then, one day, after another lovely session with Mr M Pathy, I got home and my wife announced that she was leaving. She said that I never did anything, that I carried on as if marriage was a burden and I was totally wrapped up in myself, and that this had become even worse since I had been having psychotherapy with Mr M Pathy. A great turbulence passed through my whole being. I could not sleep that night, and my wife's words kept ringing in my ears. I was in a panic: I did not want her to leave. In a dream that night, I kept hearing the name "Mr E Fective". I awoke in a cold sweat, reached for the telephone book, and looked up the name Fective. Ah, yes, there it was: E Fective, 100 Dynamic Road. I rang up and luckily got straight through to him. Could I come and see him that day? He offered me an appointment for the next morning.

There are no tapes of this session, but it had such a strong impact upon me that its quality was burned into my memory.

"I am in a terrible state. My wife is going to leave me and . . ."

Before I had a chance to say anything more Mr E Fective interrupted:

"What have you done to bring her to such a pass?"

"Well, she told me that things have been going from bad to worse since I have been seeing my psychotherapist, Mr M Pathy . . ."

And again he interrupted:

"It is because she felt that you and Mr M Pathy were ganging up against her."

I stammered,

"But . . . I did complain about her and Mr M Pathy sympathized with me, but I never said anything to her about it".

Then, to my amazement, he turned up his lips in a vicious hateful scowl. I backed away, making for the door.

"Why are you leaving so suddenly?"

"I can see you hate me."

"I have not *said* anything yet."

"No, but you put on a dreadful scowl."

"You say you did not say anything to your wife?"

"But I did not scowl at her like that."

"No, but when you returned from those sessions with Mr M Pathy, you were in a moody turn of mind and were turned off from your wife. So she felt even more hated by you than usual, just like you felt hated by me now."

I dropped into a silence for about five minutes, and then I said:

"But she always ignored me and did not treat me as a person . . ."

"But when I scowled, you were just about to leave the room. You weren't treating me with the respect deserved by a person. These interactions are two-way. She did not treat you as a person because you did not treat her as one . . ."

"But it is not just her. I wasn't treated as a person when I was a child. My mother was always nagging me."

"So this attitude of yours, that has contributed to a bad situation arising between you and your wife, goes back a long way. It is an emotional attitude that was there in childhood."

"Are you on my side or not?"

"I had the idea from the way you came in that you were very distressed, that your wife was leaving you, and that you wanted my help to do something about it."

"That's true."

"Well, I am trying to help you."

And suddenly the truth of what he said hit me between the eyes. In crisis, I caught a glimpse of things from a totally new perspective. I was appalled by it, but it gave me hope.

* * *

"Self" is a word endowed with many meanings. The following is Brian Muir's definition: "The self can be thought of as a psychological structure that contains within it the various processes of mental life."

Every definition draws a boundary so that some concepts or phenomena are included in it and others are excluded. I think we can infer from Brian's comments about object relations theory that psychological structure refers to the internal relation between the ego and objects. I take it also that under "processes" he would include drives with a source, I presume, in the *id*. Brian's definition, then, is capable of embracing Freud's Structural Model.

One of the maladies within the psychotherapeutic and psychoanalytic world is the emotional attachment that practitioners have to one clinician or another. One person is attached to Melanie

Klein and will hear not a word of criticism about her; another's bond is to Kohut, and any criticism of him is taken as an personal attack. I mention only two, but we all have our heroes, whether it be Winnicott, Bion, Fairbairn, Balint, Mahler, or Lacan. The extent to which this emotional attachment reigns supreme exactly dictates the extent to which any scientific discussion is obliterated. I hope that what I have to say in this chapter gives rise to some good, hard-headed, and objective thinking, based upon understanding and not on prejudice, and born of emotional attachment rather than scientific deduction and observation.

Brian's definition of the self encircles the ego and internal objects, whereas the self as defined by Kohut is a substitute for the ego and internal objects and is akin to a psychic wax that takes on the impression of the characters of the parents. The stress that Kohut puts on the formative nature of the psychopathology of the parents as opposed to that of isolated traumatic events was well overdue in the United States. However, his belief that narcissistic disorders are caused entirely by empathic failure on the part of parents was one-sided. The personality of the child would be affected in much the same way that a seal makes an impression upon wax. His view is a deterministic one that is indistinguishable from that of J. B. Watson or Skinner. Classical psychoanalysis suffers from a narrow determinist theory of causality, and, strange to say, despite all the clamour of Kohut's disciples against drive theory and classical analysis, their clinical perspective is based upon it. Although Kohut set out to replace Hartmann's model, in reality he only pasted his conceptualization of the self over it.

We can at first sight be glad that Kohut set out to humanize the mechanistic theory bequeathed to the United States by Hartmann, but the best intentions can go wrong if they are not rooted in the right soil. So it is with Kohut: all his theories are based upon a belief in primary narcissism. I will explain what this means. Kohut assumes that the infant, at the earliest stage, exists in an objectless medium of sheer bliss: the image for this state of affairs is the foetus floating in utter contentment in the amniotic fluid. Early analysts such as Ferenczi believed that this state, encoded in the archaic memory, was responsible for mankind's regressive longing for paradise. We now know that the idea that all is bliss in

the womb is fantasy and that, in reality, the human being, during the foetal stage of development, suffers all the favours and reverses of fortune with which we become familiar in later life.

Quite a number of analysts of the object relations school also held the theory of primary narcissism, but the difference between them and Kohut was that the latter made it the foundation stone of his personality theory. I will quote a short passage from *The Analysis of the Self*.

> The equilibrium of primary narcissism is disturbed by the unavoidable shortcomings of maternal care, but the child replaces the previous perfection (a) by establishing a grandiose and exhibitionistic image of the self, the *grandiose self*; and (b) by giving over the previous perfection to an admired, omnipotent (transitional) self-object, the *idealized parent imago*. [Kohut, 1971, p.25]

This lies at the very heart of his theoretical and clinical formulations. A failure in maternal care, an empathic failure, disturbs the equilibrium of primary narcissism which must immediately be restored. You may note here that, like Hartmann, he is firmly wedded to the homeostatic theory of motivation in which the human being immediately seeks to remedy a tension state or disequilibrium. This was Freud's earliest instinct model of motivation. I doubt that any European analyst would still seriously espouse the homeostatic theory, yet a vast school of clinicians—the self psychologists—base themselves upon it. When I use the term "European analyst", I mean those who have been influenced by the philosophical school of thought represented by such figures as Vico, Herder, Hamann, Kant, Kierkegaard, Heidegger, Merleau-Ponty, Macmurray, Collingwood, or more contemporary hermeneutic sociology. These all challenged, in their different ways, the positivism that underpins Kohut's psychology and most of psychoanalysis in America. Brian raises a very challenging question when he asks: "Could it be that the Kohut school is but one manifestation of a much wider and more insidious phenomenon in Western, and particularly North American culture: a shallowness of values and the pursuit of a naive humanistic ameliorism?"

"They can't all be wrong!", I hear you say. Most of us will accept a *folie à deux*: Erich Fromm (1972, p. 16) drew attention to the alarming phenomenon of a *folie à millions* and cited Nazi Germany as a prime example.

I would like to draw your attention to the fact that Bion took a contrary view: that the infant has a choice—either to evade frustration or to modify it. Therefore, the establishment of a *grandiose self* is not a *necessary* consequence of failure in maternal care. I want to draw attention also to the fact that, whereas Kohut says that the grandiose self *is* a necessary consequence of empathic failure, Bion (1962, p. 29) says it results from a decision to avoid frustration. Isaiah Berlin (1979, pp. 25–75) said that Macchiavelli caused a scandal in the Middle Ages, not because he recommended that a prince needed to be ruthless if he was to rule well, but because he faced his audience with a choice: either to be a successful prince, which required a good dose of ruthlessness, or to follow the Christian virtues of humility and meekness. It was the choice he faced them with that caused such a scandal. You have a Machiavelli in front of you at the moment: you have a choice to make between these two views. Either one sees human beings as being compelled to reinstate the equilibrium, or one sees them trying to avoid frustration or, if it cannot be avoided, bearing it and modifying it. If, as a psychotherapist, you take the first of these two choices, then you will believe that you can cure people by redressing the balance first upset by the patient's parents. If you take the second view, then you believe that the mind is healed through truth.

So Kohut says that, in the face of empathic failure, the child substitutes the previous perfection with the establishment of a grandiose self, which, he believes, is a satisfactory way of managing these frustrating empathic failures. Now, analysts of the Kleinian school especially, but also most analysts in London of the other two schools—the Classical Freudian school and the Independent Group—have as an aim the transformation of the grandiose self. Omnipotence is judged to be a bad thing, but why is that so? Am I not perfectly free to be omnipotent if I so wish? To answer such a question, I would ask you to imagine the following scene. A patient comes to see me because he keeps falling in love with women who shortly leave him for other men. One day I point out his omnipotence, so he asks me if he is not perfectly free to be omnipotent. I reply that of course he is free to be omnipotent, but if that is what he wishes, I cannot help him. The reason is that, through the grandiose self, he blows away his jealousy, and women soon leave him for men who desire them. It is through omnipotence that one hallucinates, distorts one's perceptions, obliterates memory, sabotages thought, banishes guilt, and substitutes fantasy for reality. Through omnipotence, the processes of the mind and the mind's objects are destroyed.

Kohut does not see any of this. He substitutes the grandiose self for the paradise of primary narcissism, but because he does not see the *activity* of omnipotence he believes that it is a satisfactory exchange. But it is through omnipotence that the activities of the mind are obliterated. Yet, as the mind is activity, the conclusion must be that Kohut's clinical system is anti-mind. (I am only repeating here Brian's statement that Kohut misses out a whole dimension of psychic life.) This is because the mind is a system of activities. The self of self psychology has been left with sensuousness and feelings, but it has obliterated the higher mental activities.

In Kohut's system, the infant evades frustration by exchanging an idealized self-object—parent imago—for the previous perfection. The idealized self-object functions in an empathic way towards the grandiose self. The grandiose self *demands* an idealized self-object—the two are linked together. If I function as a self-object for a patient (or for anyone else for that matter), then I have given up my own freedom and agreed to be the empathic endorser of the grandiose self of the other. In my own intrapyschic world, my free-thinking individual self has been obliterated. (I have frequently supervised people whose own feelings have been totally obliterated in such a process.)

Kohut's definition of the self excludes an active emotional ego, it excludes the reality of "the other", and it excludes drives. On the other hand, Brian Muir has given us an inclusive definition of the self. His definition includes a place for drives and an active ego and allows for a perception of the other—and, most important of all, it includes the mind. Kohut's self excludes it. Brian's conceptualization of the self is more profound, more complex and more all-embracing than that of Kohut. Although it would take much time and effort to teach it, the result would be well worth while.

* * *

Both the vignettes at the start of this chapter and the discussion above should illuminate just what it is about Brian's conception of the self which goes beyond Kohut's. The difference between the two vignettes is that Mr M Pathy takes the view that his patient is a passive victim of events, both present and past, whereas Mr E Fective sees his patient as an active agent. I follow the view of the philosopher, Edmund Husserl (1973), who said:

> This phenomenologically necessary concept of receptivity is in no way exclusively opposed to that of the *activity of the ego*, under which all acts proceeding in a specific way from the ego-pole are to be included. On the contrary, receptivity must be regarded as the lowest level of activity. The ego consents to what is coming and takes it in. [p. 79]

Kohut's view, as I have said, is that narcissistic disorders are caused by empathic failure on the part of parents, and I have claimed that this is a view that is, in effect, indistinguishable from that of J. B. Watson or Skinner. Classical psychoanalysis suffers from a narrow determinist theory of causality. I am quite open to this view, but disciples of Kohut need to show me *how* this receptivity occurs—I am certainly not prejudiced against a theory just because it is old.

What needs to be shown is how the empathic failure of parents affects the child. What is the process of internalization? How does the empathic attunement of a psychotherapist reverse this "bad internalization"? You may think that the first vignette I gave is a vulgar caricature of the kind of therapy that results from this "seal and wax" theory. It is a fiction, but nevertheless it is representative of the therapeutic style of many psychotherapists which does not allow for the composite inner structure of the personality. I think that Brian Muir's definition of the self is a very comprehensive one: "The self can be thought of as a psychological structure that contains within it the various processes of mental life." Such a definition is not restrictive and allows for the activity of the ego. The Kohutian definition of the self is oppositional to the ego.

I have emphasized throughout that Kohut's intentions were good: he wanted to humanize the mechanistic ego-psychology in the United States. However, to transform a theory requires radical re-thinking, and this Kohut did not do. The therapy that results from his theory changes the presented self. Internalization and change of structure require me to understand those emotional activities that have their source in me. This is a painful process, but it leads to lasting change in the personality.

In the first vignette, the patient *felt* better, but it was at a surface level. In the crisis that confronted him when his wife was going to leave him, he was thrown back upon his deeper feelings. You might ask where these feelings were before. I think the answer is that he was hypnotized *to* the psychotherapist and thereby cut off from his deeper feelings. The psychotherapist *was* the patient's self-object. In Kohut's theory, the selfobject is a narcissistic creation, and, in that situation, the individual is in contact with neither his own inner person nor that of the psychotherapist.

Conclusion

The question revolves around this point: what is the aim of therapy? Does it aim to make me feel good and whole, or is it to equip me to manage the crises of my life? To this question, there follows another. What ultimately is it that strengthens the self, that enables the self to ride the emotional storms? What factor is it in the self that raises inner self-esteem? Jung (1933, p. 270) said: "The patient does not feel himself accepted unless the very worst in him is accepted, too."

All aspects of the self need to be accepted: the loving and the hating, the good and the bad, the admired and the despised. I think the big lacuna in Kohut's theory is his failure to ascribe emotional activity to the self. Within the human race there are Hitlers, capable of massive destructiveness, and Mother Teresas, capable of great constructive purposes. These capacities also exist within us. I hold the view that the goal of therapy is to free the constructive desire and to sublimate destructiveness within that purpose.

I would like to end by reminding you that the self has been conceptualized in many different ways. Kohut's is only one way, and it is one from which rigorous thought is painfully absent. I think that the intellectual and emotional work that needs to be done is to take Kohut's good intentions and re-root them in a new theoretical foundation. This is a very big undertaking, but I hope that my development of Brian Muir's arguments will provoke thoughtful debate to this end.

CHAPTER FIFTEEN

A question of conscience

This chapter is based on two papers, "Conscience and the Superego" and "Conscience and the Good", in which I examine that part of a person's inner emotional agency that we call conscience and its integration in the personality.

I begin with a simple statement. It is this: that when a patient follows his conscience, his ego is strengthened. It was very surprising for me when I realized that. It was an unexpected discovery, and yet I think it is an ancient truth, a truth that predates psychoanalysis by more than a couple of millennia. This truth was stated with stark clarity by Plato in *The Gorgias*. I need now to explore and go a bit more deeply into what I mean when I say that the patient decides to follow his own conscience.

When I say that a patient follows his own conscience, I am talking about a particular action in his inner emotional life that has external repercussions on those people with whom he is emotionally engaged. The kind of action I am talking about is a psychic action. I need now to give you an example.

I was once treating a girl who was a secretary to a man in a large business organization. Her boss, whom we shall call Mr

Smith, treated her in a patronizing, exploitative way. As time went on, I found she would miss sessions quite often and insisted that I see her early in the morning, because no other time was possible. Then she could not pay me the normal fee, and she didn't tell me things that were essential for me to know if I were to perform effectively as an analyst. One day, I was sitting there listening to what she was saying about Mr Smith, and it came home to me that she was treating me with the same contempt of which she accused Mr Smith. I might mention that this realization did not come all at once, but bit by bit until the picture became clear. So, bit by bit, I pointed out to her the way she was treating me. For a long time she repudiated these interpretations of mine, until in one session, when I made the point with more poignancy than I had done before, she became silent. I felt certain that she had taken in what I had just said and was pondering on it, whereas in the past she had dismissed it peremptorily and with great indignation.

At our next session, she told me that at work the previous day, Mr Smith had been benign towards her. He had made a point of letting her go at half past five, rather than hold her back as he usually did without pay for another hour or two. He had said please and thank you. She had never experienced such behaviour from him before. I intuited that what she reported was directly connected with my interpretation of the day before. At the time, this came as a surprise to me, as I was a newly qualified analyst. However, since then, I have had numerous similar experiences—in fact, so much so, that it is almost possible to predict what may occur.

What I want to investigate now is what exactly occurred—what was the link between my interpretation on Tuesday and her report of Mr Smith's benign behaviour towards her the following day?

Conscience and the superego

My reconstruction of the events so far described is as follows. My interpretation confronted her with what she had been doing, of which she had been quite unconscious until then. She had been treating someone in a disrespectful and patronizing way: this someone happened to be me. The source of this behaviour was her ego (I am taking as accepted the notion that the source of action in the personality is the ego). When an action is destructive, self-defeating, emotionally damaging to self and others, or emotionally cruel or vengeful, it is very frequently unconscious. It is also clear that, when the ego acts in this way, the individual expects retaliation. The agent of retaliation in the personality is what Freud described as the *superego*. I want to describe how this functions.

One thing I noticed with my patient was that, although she had the most fearsome superego, she either had no conscience at all or had one that was operating very feebly. I think that, when I made the interpretation and she silently took it in, that taking in of the interpretation was an activity of the ego. My clinical experience confirms Husserl's (1948) view that the ego is always active: an impression is not made *upon* the ego—the ego consents to *receive* such an impression. I believe, therefore, that what occurred at that moment was that the ego received the gestalt described by the interpretation. This is an action contrary to the previous one, in which the ego pushed the gestalt out and into the unfortunate Mr Smith.

The ego is always active—it either takes in or pushes out. When it pushes out, it does so into a figure in the person's emotional environment. The persecuting superego is incarnate in an individual. The persecution is experienced as coming from the individual with whom there is some emotional link, or the national or group representative of such an individual. I need to stress at this point that this defensive action on the part of the ego also affects the person who becomes the receiver of the projection. It is also a fact that individuals usually select for such a projective process a good candidate. So the day after my interpretation, my patient remained receptive of the gestalt and did not push it out—

her experience of Mr Smith was therefore a different one. When the ego propels away a hateful part of itself, this distorts perception of the external environment. It not only distorts it but cajoles the environment into conforming to that distortion.

Now the ego has only two options: it can either push out—project the gestalt—or start to do something. The point I want to make is that, in this case, when the patient actively received my interpretation, a decision was taken not to push out. She started to treat me differently, with more respect. Now I want to put this to you. What was my interpretation other than the voice of conscience? And when she decided to do something, she had decided to follow her conscience rather than thrust away its disturbing voice and hating it in the unfortunate Mr Smith.

The subsequent course of events with this patient was a slow increase in the degree to which she followed her conscience and a decrease in the intensity of her superego. This was manifest in many ways. When she came to me, she was far too terror-struck to be able to contemplate driving a car; she was terrified of swimming, she had no boyfriends, and she was the dogsbody in her office. She shared a bedsitter with two other girls and had to suffer them pushing her out into the local coffee shop when they had their boyfriends in. At the end of her analysis, she could drive a car, went snorkelling, was director of a large research organization, and, finally, about a year after the end of her analysis, she married. I mention these purely to illustrate that her ego was far stronger. It was noticeable in her analysis that her superego reduced in tandem with her increased attention to conscience.

There are two points that need further elaboration. The first concerns the way in which the evacuatory actions of the ego fashion the superego, and the second concerns the psychological nature of conscience.

The avoidance of self-knowledge

It is in order to avoid knowledge that the ego evacuates. In order not to know, the ego dissociates from this part. The ego is able to take up a psychological stance of rejection of part of its own structure and then shit it out into an external figure. It is the reason one frequently hears this sort of remark: "Oh, heavens, why is Susie shacked up with such a foul bloke. She's such a nice girl and Bob is such a bastard." When Susie shits it out she has to have a toilet and hence Bob. When she shits out this dissociated part and thrusts it into Bob, she thereby makes the superego. She has to do this because to have the superego within is far too frightening. If she has it within, it may order her to kill herself. This is because the very act of disowning and projecting increases guilt. It is a very dangerous moment in an analysis when the patient takes the superego back into the self, for exactly that reason: it may order her to commit suicide.

The psychological nature of conscience

Whether conscience functions consciously or unconsciously depends upon the extent of integration in the personality at any one time. For conscience to function consciously, it is necessary for the personality to have achieved a certain degree of integration. In its absence, conscience is destroyed and replaced with a fierce superego. Some patients come for psychoanalysis without a functioning conscience, being ruled instead by a tyrannical superego. Establishment of conscience coincides with integration of the self, and this coincides with conscience becoming conscious. The question of how this transformation takes place is a subject in its own right, but the briefest resume now follows.

A state of unintegration is kept in being through the power of a disintegrative force; there is no conscience but, instead, a fierce superego. When there are only traces of integration, there is no conscience. Conscience is an organ of consciousness. The superego directs its attacks towards the movements of integration within the unconscious. This superego is unconscious; the possessor of it is not aware that it is within him because he projects it out into another, usually an authority figure. The prison that houses the demon and superego in a vice-like grip ensures no change—there is no mind in such a situation as everything is evacuated. The demon who controls the core of the personality offers the superego deferential offerings to keep it at bay. I believe it would be very helpful if it were possible to know the ingredients that are necessary for this transformation.

The transformation of superego into conscience cannot be considered just on its own. The change is one of the by-products of a more all-embracing transformation. The ingredients of the unconscious are undifferentiated. They are jammed up and fused, and the whole ensemble is governed by the forces of the pleasure principle—what is uncomfortable is expelled, and what is comforting is selected. The individual is unconsciously ruled by this principle. What I refer to as the demon is the figure that maintains the structure in this way. The projected superego is the external representation of this.

When the elements are undifferentiated and jammed up and under the sway of projective and introjective mechanisms, there cannot be awareness. It is wrong to conceptualize it such that the elements of consciousness exist in the same way in the unconscious, and it only requires the status of consciousness for them to become conscious. The elements are held not only jammed into each other, but they are also under the sway of the forces of the pleasure principle. There is a constant interplay between these two forces which reign supreme. Knowingness is a function of parts of the self integrating. Unknowingness is a function of the elements disintegrating. Together with parts integrating goes differentiation. Integration means "relation-to" between parts. "Relation-to" allows differentiation which allows awareness. It is the differentiated object that opens awareness. In the area of unawareness, the pleasure principle reigns supreme; in the area of awareness or consciousness, the reality principle reigns.

The "Voice of Conscience" is the speech of the integrated part of the self addressing the actions of the unintegrated part. The unintegrated part does not emotionally register the presence of a person. Conscience is therefore a challenge to integration: the integrated part of the personality challenges the unintegrated. There is a power within that either disintegrates or maintains unintegration. Specifically, conscience speaks for the integrated part and counsels it not to join forces with the disintegrative power. Conscience "speaks", digs the doer in the ribs, but, if the agent acts in accord with the voice, it no longer exists as an "outsider" within. The voice of conscience is incorporated and becomes, through a piece of intentional action, an established piece of character—it becomes an ego-structure. But, if banished, conscience turns into the superego, which then persecutes the ego. So the ego is either strengthened or weakened according to the action. Neutrality in relation to conscience is not possible. Conscience is a catalyst within the personality that leads either upwards to nobility of character or downwards to moral degradation. If the ego acts against conscience it can only do so by banishing conscience. Banishing means breaking up the parts that constitute conscience through their coherence.

There is a tendency in a man for a clouding of the issues. Tolstoy describes this well in an incident in *War and Peace* (1865–1868). Early on in the novel (p. 33), Pierre gives his word of honour to Prince Andrei that he will not go to Kuragin's dissipated party. However, as he is driving home, a passionate desire comes over him to go for one last time to Kuragin's; he tells himself that his word to Prince Andrei was not binding because before he had given it he had already promised Kuragin he would go. Hence the truth of what he had seen was obscured with a subterfuge. John Steiner wrote a paper entitled "Turning a Blind Eye" (1985) in which he describes this phenomenon. It is that the clear field, upon which conscience is able to illuminate for the individual the path of righteousness, is obscured. The way this obscuring takes place can be seen in this incident from *War and Peace*.

Just before Pierre gives his word to Prince Andrei, he has said, "Seriously, I have been thinking of it for a long time. . . . Leading this sort of existence I can't decide or think properly about anything. One's head aches and one spends all one's money. He invited me this evening but I won't go." Then Tolstoy writes that a passionate urge came over him. So it is the passionate urge that obscures by forcing reason to conform to its aims. What is to be understood by this passionate urge? There was in this case a pull towards women, drink, and sensuality. There is the sense about it that it is against the judgements of his better self. What is the origin of such an urge?

I believe that the person who has best given an answer to this question is the psychoanalyst Fairbairn. He says (1958) that what each individual most deeply seeks is emotional contact with another and that this gives meaning to life. When this is blocked, substitute gratifications are sought, but they are ultimately unsatisfying. Frances Tustin (1981) believes that the origin of autism, which is fundamentally a cutting-off from emotional contact, derives from a premature separation of the infant from mother which is traumatic. I believe both these views give half the story. The other half is supplied by Melanie Klein and some of her followers. I think particularly of Leslie Sohn (1985), who posits that a narcissistic condition derives from an envious impulse. I believe that these traumata, described by Fairbairn and Tustin, open the floodgates to this envious impulse. Therefore, Pierre's "passionate urge" was a tributary of this envious impulse. The envious impulse takes on the character pattern of the object that has brought about the trauma. Against the passionate urge, the envious impulse, is the small clear voice, the voice we call conscience.

Conscience and the good

The task of the religious originator is to sound the voice of conscience loudly by setting the options out clearly. As has already been pointed out in the chapter on narcissism (chapter ten), it seems clear that every baby is subject to the envious impulse. If it is correct that it is set loose by emotional failure in upbringing, then no rearing is so perfect that this is avoided. However, the degree to which this will be active varies greatly. Sometimes people with severe trauma in childhood seem relatively free of it, whereas another person who apparently comes from a "good home" is loaded with mental disturbance. No one is free of it, however, and this accounts for what has been called Original Sin or the "Condition of Man". It is to this general state of mankind that religious originators address themselves.

The illuminator of conscience

The question is whether the choice directed by conscience is articulated by an outer object or whether it is purely subjective. The Russian moral philosopher Vladimir Solovyof poses the problem of our denying that there is any outer object that corresponds to the choice directed by conscience. If we deny that there is, then we are faced with one of two alternatives: *moral amorphism* or *passive submission*. In the first case, the individual decides just through his own subjective feeling: in the latter, he submits to an external authority usually embodied in an institution. Solovyof (1918) points out that both these views err for the same reason:

> The two opposed views coincide in the fact that neither of them take the good in its essence, or as it is in itself, but connect it with acts and relations which may be either good or evil according to their motive and their end. In other words, they take something which is good, but which may become evil, and they put it in the place of the Good itself, treating the conditioned as the unconditional. [p. xxviii]

What Solovyof is saying is that the Good is a real object. I am adding to this by saying that it is the object that illuminates conscience. It is therefore the object that governs practical judgement rather than the assent to truth. The latter can be divorced from practical judgement. I will give an example.

I am in London reading a travel book about Australia. In it I read that in the Sydney Basin there are numerous funnel web spiders, which sometimes attack human beings and kill them. I have never been to Australia, and I assent to the truth of this statement but it does not touch me. Australia is 12,000 miles away on the other side of the globe and I am never likely to go, although it is true that my old aunt Jesse lives there and comes to London every other year or so. I think no further about it, but the next day I get an urgent fax from Aunt Jesse asking me to come to Sydney straight away because she has to undergo a serious operation and badly wants to see me. Then, with anxiety, I remember about the funnel web spiders. Perhaps I shall be risking death to go to Sydney. Shall I go or shall I not? This is now a practical matter. Being very fearful of death, I shrink from going to so dangerous a place, but the voice of conscience starts sounding in my head. Aunt Jesse has always loved me and has been exceptionally good to me. Conscience sounds louder. Although still afraid, I decide to go to Sydney, and I book a plane the next day.

Truth invites intellectual assent: the Good solicits practical judgement. Truth finds its inner subjective representative in assent: the inner representative of the Good is conscience.

The concept of Good and the meaning of life

The Good is a concept used to describe a psychosocial reality. Other concepts of this nature would be Truth, Friendship, or Projective Identification, to mention just three. Such a concept has an inner and outer component. The inner component of the Good is conscience, and the outer is located outside of the self. It may be asked, where is this located? It is quality of being discernible by the human mind. Just as one colour can be differentiated from another, so the Good is a quality of being that is capable of being distinguished by the mind through the workings of conscience. The Good outside with its representative within forms a single structure. The Good, however, makes sense only if it is understood that the meaning of life is to be found in the choice of the Absolute, best described by Kierkegaard.

Kierkegaard (1843, pp. 167–169) says that before the individual decides to make a choice of good rather than evil, there is a more radical choice. It is to be in the arena of wanting to make that choice. It is what he calls the ethical as opposed to the aesthetic. A person decides that the meaning of life is in the ethical—to be in the arena of good and evil. The meaning of life unfolds from within this option like a chicken out of an egg. According to this concept, the meaning of life lies in this radical choice. In opposition to this, the meaning of life is held to lie in the satisfaction of needs, registered as pleasure. This is hedonism, the pleasure principle, the principle of constancy or the homeostatic theory of motivation. Freud held the view that we are all born under the sway of the pleasure principle, but we are challenged to take account of the reality principle. We can avoid the latter, but, if we do, it leads to mental disturbance.

The aesthete, then, stays within the motivating force of the pleasure principle and the ego remains a passive object. To be swayed by the reality principle is to respond to the human world in which the individual is placed. Freud's developmental psychology turned on the axis of the demands that the reality principle places upon the human psyche. The decision to meet the challenge of reality is a religious decision. Freud was demanding a religious decision but did not use such a language. The meaning of life for him was not that of the aesthete.

For the aesthete, the meaning of life is based upon a state of affairs, upon the satisfaction of needs. The mental processes are servants to these needs. And in this state of affairs there is a refusal to meet a reality that transcends the circumference of the self. The aesthete's goals are to enjoy life, to live life to the full, to seek excitement, to fulfil the self. Goals are ordered to satisfy the needs of the self.

Kierkegaard argues that the goals of the aesthete are encompassed within the radical choice of the ethical personality, but not vice versa. This radical choice or option catapults the individual onto the stage of Good and Evil. Evil is constituted by all those "need" elements that drag at the individual and pull him away from the call of the Good in conscience. Evil is not in the needs themselves but in the psyche's attachment to them. Psychoanalysis has illuminated these need attachments. I will give an example.

A boy was much attached to his mother. His attachment to her was not to her person but to certain sensations and images. He lived in her erotic yearnings. He liked roast chicken, but not boiled; he did not like pears; he liked Italy, but not France; he liked dry wines, but not sweet; he liked opera, but not ballet; he liked impressionist paintings, but not post-impressionist. All these likes and dislikes were dictated by his feelings. When enveloped by these feelings, he lived in a "sensation-Mummy", although now he was an adult. It shielded him from the tragic sadness of having lost Mummy. By living within this shield and making the world cater to this desire, he protected himself from the loss and his subsequent hard and bitter feelings about the loss. His real mother he did not know, nor did he know any person. He only knew them insofar as they stimulated pleasant or unpleasant feelings. This sensation-Mummy was evil in that it seduced him away from himself and from others. It seduced him away from the Good in conscience.

Conscious perception and emotional registration

In mature religion, man is saved through placing conscience as his supreme guide for action. The voice of conscience summons the individual to act in a way that is contrary to that which he is intending. Conscience bids the individual to act with respect towards his fellows. The voice of conscience sounds when the individual is about to violate this respect. Respect for the other is the natural outcome of the emotional registration of the presence of the other as person, and the capacity to register this presence depends upon the integrity of the self. Pursuit of the good is the action that integrates the self.

There is a difference between conscious perception and emotional registration. In conscious perception, an individual takes in the fact that a figure in the perceptual field is a person. He will be able to address him as such. He can write him a letter and put his name on the envelope. He knows that he is a person. While this is true at the level of the presentation of the self, where social interaction takes place, yet he does not register this at the emotional level. At this level, he is an object, not a person. This distinction is determined by the intentional act. When the inner state is disintegrated, the activity of the self is in the service of holding the parts together. The self then uses the human beings in its environment as objects to fulfil this role, but it does not perceive these humans emotionally as people.

The inner structural situation is usually a divided one, so that even in a disintegrated state there will be occasional flashes of unified action in which there is emotional perception of the person. There are, then, two movements in conflict with one another within the individual: there is action to maintain the inner status quo, and there is, at the same time, a desire to integrate. The emotional registration of the other as person or object depends upon which of these two activities of the psyche is operating at the time.

Conclusion

In this chapter, I have wanted to establish the point that ego-strength is built up each time someone follows conscience. If our task is to strengthen the ego so that it can manage better the emotional crises of life, and if what I have observed is true, then an understanding of conscience becomes crucial for the psycho-therapist. I have further tried to differentiate between conscience and an archaic superego. When Freud talks of the superego, he sometimes means something similar to conscience as I describe it here, but towards the end of his life he described the superego as the seat of destructive and anti-life forces. I am using superego in this latter sense here and differentiating it from conscience. Recognizing the difference between these two agencies within the personality is crucial for any working psychotherapist.

CHAPTER SIXTEEN

Psychotherapy and religion

I believe that the psychotherapy movement is experiencing a period of severe crisis, a crisis that is similar to and with the same roots as the crisis that is evident in organized religion throughout the Western world. I wish therefore in this chapter to start by presenting the view that the contemporary psychotherapy movement (i.e. the movement that has developed since the days of Freud) developed as a reaction to the dominant attitudes within organized religion. From there I want to go on to examine what I call traditional religion and its categories. I then go on a brief excursus into the symbolic nature of the sexual and, from there, to an examination of conscience and its formative role in mental health. This leads naturally to an examination of the great religious teachers as illuminators of conscience, and then to my view that the crisis in the psychotherapy movement lies in the philosophical nominalism that underpins it. I shall end by trying to adumbrate the hazy outline of a solution—a solution that lies in the development of a concept of the Good within the sphere of human intimacy. I should add that the reader may notice certain similarities between this chapter and the previous one in viewpoints argued and concepts presented. However, the excision of such overlap in either chapter would have resulted in a dilution of what I am trying to say.

The psychotherapy movement as a reaction against puritanism

The psychotherapy movement is a violent protest against Calvinistic religion. We are all familiar with the moral strictures of the Victorian Age. These strictures reached an alarming severity in all matters pertaining to sex. It was, for instance, extremely shameful when an unmarried girl became pregnant. No author has portrayed these attitudes with greater poignancy than Thomas Hardy in his descriptions of the pain and agony of people, especially women, following on any such misdemeanour. He also described the appalling psychological prisons in which decent people were forced to live in that era. Thomas Hardy was writing about the social scene in rural England in the last decades of the nineteenth century. It is important to remember that Hardy only died in 1928. Feminist literature has emphasized the way in which women in particular were the victims of these strictures, with the obvious implication of a double standard, of hypocrisy. The meaning of this was that the moral errors of the accusers were perhaps worse than the misdemeanours of the condemned. This was also well portrayed earlier in the nineteenth century by the American author Nathaniel Hawthorne, in his novel *The Scarlet Letter*. He described the severe condemnation of the protagonist, Hester Prynne, while the clergyman who had made her pregnant escaped free of stricture. Reading about the strict puritanical morality that haunted those New England communities can even today give us a chill running down the spine.

The originator of this severe piety was, with little doubt, John Calvin. His theocratic rule in Geneva would be hard to believe were it not for the fact that it is well documented. Calvin had what we would call today a secret police, who had the right to burst into people's private homes. When these secret police burst in upon a couple engaged in illicit sexual relations, they were declaimed, summarily charged, and led to execution. This Calvinistic religion took a firm grip upon Anglo-Saxon culture, initiated perhaps in the British Isles by John Knox, who had sat at Calvin's feet in Geneva. The way in which this puritan doctrine gripped Anglo-Saxon culture and the way it ultimately led to the accumulation of wealth and the development of a character structure has been described in a masterly way by Max Weber in his short but brilliant essay *The Protestant Ethic and the Rise of Capitalism* (1930). His penetrating understanding of the psychological consequences of this particular religious temper upon the psychology of the individual demands, I believe, our attention.

This culture was implanted in Australian soil by the people of the "First Fleet", starting in 1788. The "Protestant Ascendancy" was the most important actor on the stage in those founding years of Australian society. The early governors were all charged with establishing the Protestant Ascendancy, with its puritan morality. Governor Macquarie, like his predecessors, was charged with improving the morality of the convicts. He was commanded not to tolerate the illicit sexual liaisons that were almost the norm among the convict men and women. All inducements to ensure that convicts put away their sinful ways and entered upon the state of matrimony were to be exercised. These governors brought with them the severe piety that was then so entrenched in Anglo-Saxon culture. Governor Macquarie, too, insisted upon the due proprieties of the Protestant Ascendancy being carried out to the full, but, unlike his predecessors, he was shocked by the immoral behaviour of the army officers. He detected the hypocrisy that lay behind the obsessional focusing upon the sexual.

When the accuser condemns, he does not give reasons for his condemnation. He says "You are wrong", "You are wicked", or "You are sinful", but without indicating why. These condemnations come from a tyrant god; they are words spoken from on high, but there is no reasoning process behind them. They come, then, from that part of the personality that Freud named the *superego*. The superego has no access to a thinking process. As soon as it does, it becomes what I should prefer to call conscience—conscience is able to reason, whereas the superego is not. The condemnations that come from this savage tyrant do not reason; what may not be so readily acknowledged is that the victim gets pleasure from them. We all reel off readily enough the word "maso-chism" but do not take in its full import—that we derive pleasure from being beaten, from being persecuted. Freud said initially that this is because the individual who is being beaten identifies in-wardly with the sadist. However, in his later formulation, he pro-posed that masochism was primary. The fact being put forward is that the person who is condemned derives a secret pleasure from it. It is pleasure of a sensual kind. It is because of this pleasure that the individual has an attachment to it. He is addicted to it. The point I am making is that although it may superficially look as though sexual orgies are the opposite of this puritanical attitude, the attitudes are two sides of the same coin. This double-sided visage of what is in fact one psychological phenomenon was rec-ognized by those early Church Fathers known as the Apologists, in their disputes with the Gnostics. The Gnostics demonstrated just this duality. They swung between a puritanism of draconian severity to orgies of the most luxuriant and perverse kind. The Apologists recognized that they were up against a unitary phe-nomenon, although it displayed two different manifestations.

This extremely puritanical attitude towards sex is, as I have suggested, a recent development. It dates from Calvin and only became predominant in European culture in the seventeenth century. Philippe Aries, the historian of mentalities, has demon-strated clearly in his book *Centuries of Childhood* (1973) that a quite different social attitude prevailed prior to the seventeenth cen-tury. He quotes from the journal that recorded the early infancy of Louis XIII. The lords and ladies at court would come to look at the child, and someone would take a feather and tickle his penis, to the accompaniment of lewd jokes and roars of laughter. Such be-haviour was unthinkable a century later.

The modern movement of psychotherapy represents a violent reaction against these puritanical attitudes. Psychotherapy en-dorses a different attitude: one of understanding, of empathy, the neutral stance, one of acceptance. However, this reaction is the other side of the same coin. The psychotherapist takes up an atti-tude where he does *not* condemn or accuse his patient. He says: "I do not condemn you", "I affirm your existence", and "I accept you". However, in that there is no reasoning behind them, these words of comfort are not dissimilar to the words of those who in

earlier times condemned, though frequently there are rationaliza-
tions. The tyrant god has now become a benevolent one and wears
the face of the psychotherapist, but the tyrant does not think. It is
for this reason, I believe, that the psychotherapy movement is now
in a state of crisis. It has no goal, no direction, no meaningful
purpose. There is no concept of what mental health is. How do we
define a person who is mentally healthy? If we do not know the
answer to that, then we are surely in a parlous state.

I am, of course, taking a broad sweep and do not mean to
include everyone in the psychotherapy movement. Some individuals have attempted to rectify the situation, people like Erich
Fromm and Viktor Frankl. I exclude Jung because, although he
insisted upon the need to recognize a religious principle, he
thought that the traditional religions adequately filled that need.
You will understand, as I continue, that I do not agree with this
viewpoint. In order to understand the situation, we must turn
now and look at the religion against which the psychotherapy
movement has been in such violent protest.

The categories of traditional religion

The spirituality of traditional religion is founded upon the *fuga
mundi*—flight from the world. I differentiate traditional religion
from primitive religion, in that the latter is bounded by the demands of the survival instinct, whereas the goal of traditional
religion lies in values that transcend that instinct. These transcendent values are sought by the spiritual person in traditional
religion by taking flight from close family ties: "Let him hate his
wife and children and follow me", says Jesus. The Buddha in his
awakening left his wife and child and embraced the solitary life of
a wandering ascetic. It is probable that neither Mahavira, the
founder of Jainism, nor Zarathustra, the founder of Zoroastrian-
ism in Iran, were married. The spiritual person put aside sexual
and erotic attachment in order to concentrate upon the transcendent values. It was an inherent part of such a spirituality that it was
impossible to pursue these transcendent values whilst being in the
grip of sensual attachments. Central to these attachments is the

sexual-erotic one. We all know how sexual passion can throw us off course, blunt our perceptions, and dethrone us from our loftiest ideals. In the annals of the saints, there are many stories of monks who had to do violence to themselves in order to resist the onslaught of passionate temptation. So the gentle Saint Francis tore off his clothes and rolled in the snow, and Saint Benedict threw himself into a bramble bush when tempted to leave Subiaco and return to a woman in Rome. Buddhist monks are also bound by similar laws, by which they are not even permitted to touch a woman. This spirituality, based upon a violent repudiation of the sexual, extended beyond the genital. Erotic attachments to children, parents, brothers, and sisters had to be cut in order to make progress in the spiritual life.

Some of you may raise the objection that this is not so of some of the traditional religions. It was certainly not so of primitive religions, which are usually tribally based and hitched to the survival instinct. So, for instance, you would find none of this in the religion of the Dinka tribes in southern Sudan. There is another element that must be added in order to define traditional religion accurately. The traditional religions are those that were founded in the Axial and post-Axial era by an individual who challenged the cultic religion in which they were reared. So the Buddha challenged some of the central religious practices of Brahmanism, as also did Mahavira. Zarathustra challenged the cultic Iranian religion of his time and Jesus, as is well known, challenged the rites and sacrifices of Judaism, just as Buddha had done with Brahmanism. Buddhism is still largely racially bound, as is Hinduism. The spiritualities that have arisen in Christianity, Buddhism, or Islam are the possession of individuals who have gone on an inner journey into themselves, a journey of individual self-discovery.

I want to return now to the spirituality of the traditional religions. Only through detachment from our erotic ties is it possible to root out pride, greed, envy, jealousy, sloth, anger, and the other vices. The reason for this is that these vices are inserted into the erotic ties so inextricably that the only solution to the problem is to cut them. It is not possible within the spiritual methodology of traditional religion to extricate the vices from the erotic attachment. In a state of sexual passion, the individual believes that consummation is good for both. The whole thing, however, may be motivated by the desire to triumph over another, to insult a third party, or to injure a hated parent, or through envy of the lover's usual partner. The scope for self-deception is so enormous that the spirituality of the traditional religions had no methods with which to deal with it other than to lay down an injunction that the only way to holiness was to sever all such ties completely. This was the reason for the severe condemnations of the sexual within the traditional religions. So the simple truth is that the traditional religions had nothing to say about those most important bonds that govern the intricate webbing of human intimacy. Judaism, in its hallowing of familial ties, did not adopt the *fuga mundi* spirituality.

I have emphasized the role of sex in human relations because the sexual symbolizes the structure of the emotional, a truth that manifests itself in the consulting-room.

> In the initial assessment, a female patient told the analyst that whenever her boyfriend looked at another woman, it would so enrage her that she would cut off all relations with him. One day, after treatment had commenced, the patient arrived and saw the analyst's previous patient departing. She, who the previous day had been helpful and cooperative, was silent and resentful at the sight of the analyst with someone else. As the treatment proceeded, it emerged that it made no difference whether the other patient she glimpsed was male or female—the image (I might almost say the subliminal image) of the two figures together was enough to send her into a rage. At a later stage, the analyst noticed something more subtle—that whenever there was a very good harmony of understanding between himself and the patient, there was a sudden change of atmosphere. The good understanding vanished, but with no evident outside interference—no other patient, no break, no end of session. It happened so regularly, so predictably, that the analyst formulated that there was a third party within the personality that had been so enraged by a glimpse of the analyst and the patient together that an interference had been set up to destroy the harmony that has been achieved. (It was Jung, 1935, pp. 72–73, who first emphatically said that it was an illusion that a personality is a unitary being—we are made

up of many complexes, many personalities, within one personality.)

So we posit the existence of a jealous figure within the self that not
only messed up interpersonal communication but thought processes, perceptual processes, the capacity for judgement, and the
functioning of memory and imagination. This is what we mean
when we say that emotional factors interfere with mental processes: we are all familiar with the person whose strong intelligence is impaired through emotional factors. The sexual, then, is a
symbol of the emotional, and it is for this reason that I have emphasized it so much.

In a nutshell, it was for this reason that mental illness became
divorced from spiritual endeavour and was entrusted to doctors,
those rather weird hybrid doctors—doctors of the soul, the psyche
yatros, psychiatrists. It was because traditional religion had no
categories within which to understand it. But what sort of a job did
these alienists, this new breed of medicine man, make of the souls
of men with which, through a strange cultural accident, they had
become entrusted? Well, of course, they did and continue to do
what doctors have always done. They used the tools of their trade,
handing out medicines or making use of the surgeon's knife. This
was the situation until a new group of psychiatrists arose, who
said that it was necessary to look at the conflicts of the soul.

The self is not unitary—it is made up of different parts. Winnicott's (1960b) idea of the mother's holding is one of an environment that cements the different parts into a unity. These parts,
under stress, can fragment, as Fairbairn (1976) conceptualized.
These different parts have, as Jung emphasized, a kind of autonomy of their own. As Melanie Klein stressed, it is possible through
splitting not to know the actions of one of the parts. This is the
sphere of knowledge that is only known by the individual in relation to an erotic object, and it was to this sphere that traditional
religion had no access and so turned its back.

Selfhood appeared only in the Axial era, that epoch when
arose the spiritual giants in our world. Only through human
action directed towards transcendent values did a concept of
selfhood arise. Without this new religious orientation, human beings are thought of purely in mechanical terms. What determines

a human model is the individual acting under the influence of a transcendent value. The particular problem for psychotherapists is that the values deriving from the great religious originators are admired and looked up to in our culture; they have society's blessing, as it were. This means that for an individual to find acceptance, he has to espouse these values externally, although he may not espouse them internally. Therefore the pretender, the hypocrite, is still in a tribal situation internally. There is in such a person no self but only the appearance of a self. The self is a construction, a self-construction, that is fashioned through acting towards transcendent values through conscience.

In the very place, then, where modern man needs understanding, he could not find it within traditional religion. We must pass on now to an analysis of those components that go to make up traditional religion.

Conscience

The individual has within himself the guide to moral action. This inner principle of action is conscience. There is a tendency to confuse the superego with conscience. The psychological term "superego" is best confined to the tyrant figure that I have referred to earlier. It is dissociated from the acting centre of the self; it addresses this part of the self as an object. Conscience, on the other hand, exists partly within the intentional source. When conscience beckons, there is a desire to follow the course being prompted. The prompting is the clamour of desire in the intentional centre. It is frequently in conflict with an impulse that pulls in another, often opposite, direction, but it remains an intentional desire of the self.

The traditional religions have all had, as their guiding principle, the concept that conscience is the prime guide of moral action. In those religions with an authoritarian structure, there is less emphasis on conscience. However, even in the Catholic Church, the prime authority of conscience has been recognized by their illustrious theologians. So, for instance, Cardinal Newman (1845) said, "I would always defer first to my conscience and then to the Pope".

From what I have written so far, it would seem to be very easy to follow the right path. What need is there for a religion if all we need do in order to "walk in the paths of righteousness" is to follow our conscience? Yet we all know that it is not at all easy; that the right path may be very dark and obscure. The role of traditional religion has quite simply been to illuminate conscience: unfortunately, that has been one of the glaring failures of religions. It has nearly always been the courageous individual who has stood by his conscience, often in opposition to the dictates of formal religion. For instance, Metzger, a priest in an obscure village in Nazi Germany, preached against Hitler's aggression. He did it against the directives of the German hierarchy and was executed for it by the Gestapo. The failures of formal religion to guide conscience are too numerous and too appalling to name. Why they have so failed is a question of crucial importance, but one we shall have to leave on one side for the moment. We must be satisfied with the statement that the *role* of formal religion has been to guide conscience. Those spiritual giants who founded the great religions of the world saw their prime task as being one of illuminating the consciences of their listeners, knowing that conscience is so shrouded in darkness that it requires illumination. They were able to illuminate conscience because they had been through a deep experience of enlightenment themselves. The roots of these great religious traditions lay in the profound inner experiences of their founders.

What these spiritual giants then did was to map out a doctrine and way of life that was incorporated by the institution that they founded—the Church in the case of Jesus, the Sangha in the case of the Buddha. Conceptually, however, the guidelines that they mapped out for living a life of dedication to transcendent values was limited in two important respects. The guidelines applied in almost every area but the sexual and erotic: this complex area was to be avoided. The other limitation was that, although the guidelines included the individual within the group, there was no conceptual grasp of the personality as a composite. Therefore, there was no illumination of conscience within that sphere.

It is too big a subject to elaborate here on the reason for this particular sphere to have become so crucial for modern man. Suffice it to say that the spectacular increase in population, the

Industrial Revolution, the transition from extended to nuclear family, the rapid increase in the ratio of urban to rural dwellers, the growth of bureaucracy, the technological explosion, and the enormous growth of leisure time have altered men's way of living, so that this sphere of emotional intimacy has become the prime sphere of human activity. The conceptualization of the individual as a composite entity has become central to an understanding of man. Traditional religions have utterly failed to meet the modern crisis and failed to conceptualize the matter in a way that enables men and women to gain access to their consciences in the midst of this confusing world.

So, to come back to where we started: the psychotherapy movement revolted violently against the dictates of traditional religion, and no one could have been more vociferous in this than Sigmund Freud. This was, I am sure, because he thought that traditional religion had failed human society in the sphere that was now so crucial: the sexual/erotic. The psychotherapy movement has followed suit, with the result that the baby has been thrown out with the bath water.

The crisis of nominalism

Whereas traditional religion condemned sexual/erotic activities, the psychotherapy movement has endorsed all behaviour and its inner concomitants. It has failed utterly to illuminate conscience. I have witnessed the most barbaric exploitations of one human being by another in this sphere, and I have questioned psychotherapists about it. I have asked, "What did you feel about that?", to be greeted by a vacuous stare. The psychotherapist evidently had no feeling about it. I want to give you two examples of what I mean.

I was supervising a psychotherapist who was treating a depressed man, a forlorn individual, unsuccessful in business. While his wife, a woman of 38, was still in hospital after the birth of their first child, he started an affair. I asked the psychotherapist what he felt about that. He replied that he felt the man was depressed. I asked again what *he* felt, and he said that he felt the man felt lonely and isolated. So I then asked him what he *thought*, and he said that he thought the man had started the affair because he was so lonely. When giving me an account of the session in which the patient had revealed the affair, the psychotherapist reported that the patient had said, "I was worried by what you might think". To which the psychotherapist replied, "You felt I might condemn you for it". This statement was the equivalent of saying to the patient, "What you have done is all right by me".

To me, it was clear that the patient was troubled by what he had done, and it was the psychotherapist's job to investigate why. Later on in the session, the fact that the patient was worried about the affair emerged clearly when he said that when he had been ill two years earlier, his wife had been very supportive. It was obvious that, because he had not responded when she needed his support following the birth of their child, his conscience pricked him. The psychotherapist, however, helped him to smother his conscience rather than illuminate it. I think that if the psychotherapist had had a sense of the modes of action by which people feel good about themselves, he would not have said what he did. As it was, the patient became more depressed—his wife found him out, felt bitter, and denied him sexual relations. The situation deteriorated yet further.

* * *

I shall now give you the second example. A woman aged 36 had given birth for the first time. She was a professional woman, efficient and businesslike. She was in therapy because she had suffered anxiety attacks about a year before her pregnancy. She did not seem the maternal type, but as soon as her baby was born, the mother in her came out strongly. She was markedly different—the psychotherapist noted that she even *looked* different. The baby was born in late July. For several years, in mid-September, she and her husband had taken their estate car to France on a special expedition to buy and take back to London about twenty-five cases of Nouveau Beaujolais. The husband was putting pressure on his wife to go on their trip as usual, and to leave the baby behind with her mother. The wife was in a state of disquiet: her inner promptings were towards the baby, but the efficient businesswoman was also pressuring her.

She said to the psychotherapist,

> "Well, I decided I would go to France, but then I lay awake and sweated and couldn't sleep".

The psychotherapist said,

> "Perhaps you don't want to go to France?"

> "Oh, no, I love these trips to France. They are the highlight of the year. We have such fun."

> "Perhaps you are guilty about having fun?"

> "Oh, no, I don't think so. It was probably that I had eaten and drunk a bit too much last night. It will pass." It evidently did not occur to that psychotherapist that the mother was troubled about leaving her baby.

* * *

There is a problem that is evident in both these cases. In the first case, the psychotherapist had no idea of the importance of the man's support for his wife at the time when she was giving birth. In the second case, it did not occur to the psychotherapist that the patient's anxiety may have been due to her maternal side wanting to stay with her baby.

I have entitled this section "The Crisis of Nominalism", and you may wonder why. Nominalism was that philosophy pioneered by William of Occam in the fourteenth century. It taught that there was no integrating factor in the human domain. This is the philosophy that underlies the present state of chaos. The individual's own feeling is the only index of action: this is the individual's feeling divorced from knowledge. Conscience is knowledge and therefore requires development and illumination.

The object of conscience is the Good. Failure to conceptualize this leads to errors of two kinds. Either the Good is equated with concrete directives, or it is equated with subjective feeling. An example of the first error would be a stipulation from traditional religion: sexual intercourse is bad unless it occurs between two people who are married. The implication here is that it is good if it occurs between a married couple, but this does not take into account at all the possibility of exploitation or cruelty in sexual relations between a man and his wife. It also concretizes the concept of marriage. The other error is to make the individual's feeling the measure of goodness. Here, an individual may feel that it is good to leave his sexual partner for another and cruelly injure a third party. It is at root the same error: that the Good is concretely equated, in the first case, with a particular object and, in the second, with a particular subject.

The Good is a psychic reality which is inner and outer. Its roots inwardly exist in the conscience; in the outer world, it has a psychic existence. Without a conceptualization of the Good as an integrative force in human relations, we end in chaos. This is the state that the psychotherapy movement is in at this moment.

The relation between religion and psychotherapy

What I have been saying is that it is beyond doubt that there is a serious vacuum both in traditional religion and in the psychotherapy movement. In traditional religion, it is that there is no illumination of conscience within the sphere of the sexual/erotic. On the other hand, the focus of the psychotherapy movement has been precisely upon this sphere, but it has lacked almost entirely any illumination of conscience. So here we have an intercultural task. The question is how to go about it. I believe that the first step is a deep, continuing discussion between thinkers from the traditional religions and from the psychotherapy movement. I have no doubt that this would demand hard thinking, difficult thinking, and certainly uncomfortable thinking. I also believe that such a discussion group would need a good philosopher in its midst. Out of this would develop provisional guidelines and principles.

On the individual level, I want to point out that, in the meantime, something important can be done by psychotherapists. There is a connection between virtue and mental health. When an individual follows his conscience, he grows mentally more robust—that is a simple statement, but you may find it surprising. Yet I have seen so many examples of it that I am convinced of its truth. I am speaking in particular of conscience followed in the sphere of the sexual/erotic and would go so far as to say that when an individual is a victim in his emotional relationships, it is always a punishment for not following conscience in another emotional sphere. This will have been an unconscious action. The conclusion from this is unavoidable: that the psychotherapist has the task of illuminating conscience. He cannot do this without an inner moral principle. There is so much confusion between conscience and the superego that psychotherapists are fearful of clarifying promptings of conscience for fear of being persecuting. The difference between being persecuting and clarification of conscience is psychologically enormous. The problem is frequently exacerbated because the two are confused in the person's psychological make-up. Such cases are not rare, and it is the psychotherapist's job to unravel that confusion. This often does not happen, because the psychotherapist himself is confused in this area.

Conclusion

However, this is a work that psychotherapists could start working on. Suffice it to say that there is also within the individual an intimate relationship between religion and mental health.

The psychotherapy movement needs a religious principle if it is to pull itself out of the moral confusion in which it now exists.

Because conscience and mental health are so closely interlinked, this moral confusion is a barrier that prevents psychotherapists from doing the job they set out to do: to enhance people's mental health. I have tried to present the reasons for this statement. It is, however, only a sketch, a beginning, but I believe it is better to attempt a beginning than not begin at all.

REFERENCES

Abraham, K. (1973). *Selected Papers of Karl Abraham*. London: Hogarth Press.

Aries, P. (1973). *Centuries of Childhood*. Harmondsworth, Middlesex: Penguin Books.

Balint, M. (1968). *The Basic Fault*. London/New York: Tavistock Publications.

Berlin, I. (1979). *Against the Current*. London: Hogarth Press.

Bettelheim, B. (1977). *The Uses of Enchantment*. New York: Alfred Knopf.

Bettelheim, B. (1983). *Freud and Man's Soul*. London: Chatto & Windus, Hogarth Press.

Bion, W. R. (1953). Notes on a Theory of Schizophrenia. In: *Second Thoughts*. London: Karnac Books, 1993.

Bion, W. R. (1962). *Learning from Experience*. London: Karnac Books, 1991.

Bion, W. R. (1974). *Brazilian Lectures*. London: Karnac Books, 1990.

Bion. W. R. (1978). Clinical seminar to the Klein Group of the British Psycho-Analytical Society. Unpublished.

Bonhoeffer, D. (1970). *Ethics*. Collins: Fontana Library.

Cogniat, R. (1978). *Raoul Dufy*. Italy: Bonfini Press.

Eliot, G. (1872). *Middlemarch*. Harmondsworth, Middlesex: Penguin Books, 1975.

Fairbairn, W. R. D. (1958). On the Nature and Aims of Psychoanalytical Treatment. In *From Instinct to Self* (edited by D. E. Scharff & E. Fairbairn Sirtles). London/Northvale, NJ: Jason Aronson, 1994.

Fairbairn, W. R. D. (1976). *Psychoanalytic Studies of the Personality*. London: Routledge & Kegan Paul.

Forster, E. M. (1924). *A Passage to India*. Harmondsworth, Middlesex: Penguin Books, 1974.

Frankl, V. E. (1964). *Man's Search for Meaning*. London: Hodder & Stoughton.

Freud, S. (1914d). On the History of the Psycho-Analytic Movement. *S.E., 14*.

Freud, S. (1917e [1915]). Mourning and Melancholia. *S.E. 14*.

Freud, S. (1923a). Two Encyclopedia Articles. *S.E. 18*.

Freud, S. (1925d [1924]). *An Autobiographical Study. S.E. 20*.

Fromm, E. (1972). *Psychoanalysis and Religion*. New Haven, CT: Bantam Books.

Gosling, R. (1980). Gosling on Bion. *The Tavistock Gazette*: 22.

Guntrip, H. (1975). My Experience of Analysis with Fairbairn and Winnicott. *International Review of Psycho-Analysis, 2*: 145–156.

Heimann, P. (1950). On countertransference. In: *About Children and Children-No-Longer*. London: Tavistock, 1989.

Houselander, C. (1952). *Guilt*. London/New York: Sheed & Ward.

Husserl, E. (1948). *Experience and Judgment*. Evanston, IL: Northwestern University Press, 1973.

Jones, E. (1972). *Sigmund Freud—Life and Work, Vol. 1*. London: Hogarth Press.

Jung, C. G. (1933). *Modern Man in Search of a Soul*. London: Routledge & Kegan Paul, Ark Paperbacks, 1984.

Jung, C. G. (1935). The Tavistock Lectures. In: *The Collected Works of C. G. Jung, Vol. 18*. London: Routledge & Kegan Paul, 1976.

Jung, C. G. (1975). Archetypes and the Collective Unconscious. In: *The Collected Works of C. G. Jung, Vol. 9* (Part I). London: Routledge & Kegan Paul, 1975.

Kierkegaard, S. (1843). *Either/Or, Vol. 2*. Princeton, NJ: Princeton University Press, 1974.

Klauber, J. (1981a). *Difficulties in the Analytic Encounter*. New York/ London: Jason Aronson.

Klauber, J. (1981b). Formulating Interpretations in Clinical Psycho-analysis. In: *Difficulties in the Analytic Encounter*. New York/London: Jason Aronson.

Klein, G. (1979). *Psychoanalytic Theory*. New York: International Univerities Press.

Klein, M. (1957). Envy and Gratitude. In: *Envy and Gratitude and Other Works 1975. The Writings of Melanie Klein, Vol. 3*. London: Hogarth Press, 1975. [Reprinted London: Karnac Books, 1993.]

Kohut, (1971). *The Analysis of the Self.: A Systematic Approach to the Psychoanalytic Treatment of Narcissistic Personality Disorders*. New York: International Universities Press.

Mead, G. H. (1972). *Mind, Self and Society*. Chicago, IL/London: University of Chicago Press.

Morgan, K. (1986). *The Path of the Buddha*. Delhi: Motilal Bamarsidass.

Muir, B. (1993). The Enigma of the Self. Lecture delivered at Symposium on the Self, Sydney.

Mullen, P. E. (1991). Jealousy: The Pathology of Passion. *British Journal of Psychiatry, 158*: 593–601.

Murdoch, Iris (1978). *The Sea, The Sea*. London: Chatto & Windus.

Newman, J. H. (1845). *An Essay on the Development of Christian Doctrine*. London/New York: Sheed & Ward, 1960.

Newman, J. H. (1852). *The Idea of a University*. London/New York: Longmans, Green & Co., 1927.

Newman, J. H. (1888). *An Essay in Aid of a Grammar of Assent*. London/ New York: Longmans.

Parker, A. (1970). *The Frying Pan*. London: Hutchinson.

Reich, W. (1933). *Character Analysis*. New York: Noonday Press, 1949.

Russell, B. (1971). *The Autobiography of Bertrand Russell, Vol. 1*. London: Allen & Unwin.

Sohn, L. (1985). Narcissistic Organization, Projective Identification and the Formation of the Identificate. *International Journal of Psycho-Analysis, 66*: 201–213. Also in *Melanie Klein Today, Vol. 1* (edited by E. B. Spillius). London/New York: Routledge, 1988.

Solovyof, V. (1918). *The Justification of the Good*. London: Constable & Co.

Steiner, J. (1985). Turning a Blind Eye: The Cover-up for Oedipus. *International Review of Psycho-Analysis, 12*: 161–172.

Symington, N. (1986). *The Analytic Experience*. London: Free Association Books.

Symington, N. (1994). *Emotion and Spirit*. London: Cassell & Co.

Thompson, F. (1913). A Holocaust. In: *The Works of Francis Thompson, Vol. 2*. London: Burns & Oates Ltd.

Tolstoy, L. N. (1865–1868). *War and Peace*. Harmondsworth, Middlesex: Penguin Books, 1986.

Tustin, F. (1981). *Autistic States in Children* (pp. 15–20). London/Henley/Boston, MA: Routledge & Kegan Paul.

Vygotsky, L. S. (1934). *Thought and Language*. Cambridge, MA: MIT Press, 1975.

Weber, Max (1930). *The Protestant Ethic and the Spirit of Capitalism* (transl. Talcott Parsons). London: Allen & Unwin.

Winnicott, D. W. (1947). Hate in the Countertransference. In *Collected Papers—Through Paediatrics to Psycho-Analysis*. London: Tavistock Publications, 1958. [Reprinted London: Karnac Books, 1992.]

Winnicott, D. W. (1956). Primary Maternal Preoccupation. In: *Collected Papers—Through Paediatrics to Psycho-Analysis*. London: Tavistock Publications, 1958. [Reprinted London: Karnac Books, 1992.]

Winnicott, D. W. (1960a). Ego Distortion in Terms of True and False Self, 1960. In: *The Maturational Processes and Facilitating Environment* (pp. 140–152). London: Hogarth Press, 1965. [Reprinted London: Karnac Books, 1990.]

Winnicott, D. W. (1960b). The Theory of the Parent–Infant Relationship. In: *The Maturational Processes and the Facilitating Environment* (pp. 37–55). London: Hogarth Press, 1965. [Reprinted London: Karnac Books, 1990.]

INDEX

activity of, 176
-neurosis, 69
psychology, 13, 98
   mechanistic, 176
   rudimentary, of infant, 6
   vs. self [Kohut], 172
   as source of action in
      personality, 181
   strength, and conscience, 179,
      191
Einstein, A., 162
Eliot, G., 18, 19, 20, 21, 47
embryo mind, 162, 163
emotional contact:
   and autism, 186
   importance of, 11, 186
   with patient:
      and analyst's true self, 21
      and greed, 155
      through imagination, 35, 45
emotional mechanisms, of
      narcissistic patient, 146
emotional registration, vs.
      conscious perception,
      190–191
emotional reservoir, 68–69
emotional security, and maturity,
      103
emotional support,
      psychotherapist's need
      for, 142–144
emotional suppression, 140
empathic attunement [Kohut], 4,
      176
empathy, 4, 195
   failure of, and narcissism,
      172–174, 176
Enlightenment, 7, 8
environment, supportive, 147
   with narcissistic patient, 141–
      144
envy, 31
   in culture, 43
   and greed, 155, 157

and imagination, 43
and negative transference, 83
and religion, 197
therapist's:
   and countertransference, 93
   patient's fear of, 44
Erikson, E., 13
erotic, vs. sexual, 76
erotic attraction, defence against,
      77–78
erotic transference, 75–81, 147

Fairbairn, W. R. D., 6, 8, 98, 172
   analysis of Guntrip of, 33
   on bad inner objects, 125
   critique of Freud of, 8
   drive theory of, 8
   on emotional contact, 11, 166,
      186
   on fragmented self, 199
   on infantile dependence, 102
   moral tradition, 7
   on narcissism, 18, 186
   on inner saboteur, 1
false self, 11, 20, 133
fear, and projective identification,
      54–58
feeling registration, 24, 25
feelings:
   barriers against reaching, 29–
      33
   communication of, 23–29
   and imagination, 39
   and narcissism, 128–135
   proto-, 29–31, 34
      and feelings, 35
      and imagination, 39
   of psychoanalyst:
      and interpretation, 39
      reaching, 29–34
   unbearable, 31–32
Ferenczi, S., 13, 118, 172
Forster, E. M., 126
Francis, St., 197

superego (*continued*):
  culture, 44
  and lack of loved object, 19
  tyrannical, 181, 183
    and retaliation, 181
Symington, N., 98
Szasz, T., 7

Tavistock Clinic, xi, 30, 66, 97
termination of analysis, 71
"theory" of the mind, 21
therapist, *see* psychotherapist
therapy, *see* psychotherapy
Thompson, F., 109
Tolstoy, L. N., 185
Topographic Model of mind
      [Freud], 12
transference, 74–95, 136, 152,
      156
  defence against, 107
  delusion, 117
  development of, 107
  and embryo mind, 163
  erotic, 75–81, 147
  interpretation, 74, 95
  levels of, 95
  love, 19
  mimetic, 118–119
    analyst's point of view
      of, 119–123
  negative, 81–87
    interpretation of, 66, 67,
      86–87
    recognizing, 84–86
  neurotic, 32, 33
  psychotic, 25, 32–33
  use of, 116, 117

traumatic power of analysis,
      107–109
true self, 11, 14, 15, 20, 21, 133,
      134, 135
Tustin, F., 186

Unconscious:
  existence of, 114
  and feelings [Freud], 29
unconscious resistance, 73
  in analyst, 61
understanding, of patient, cure
      through, 99–104

"vertex", different [Bion], 4
Vico, G. B., 173
victimhood, and maturity, 102,
      103
Vygotsky, L. S., 163

Watson, J. B., 172, 176
Weber, M., 194
William of Occam, 204
Winnicott, D. W., 5–8, 13, 98, 154,
      172
  analysis of Guntrip of, 33, 34
  on child and maternal
      environment, 5–6
  on countertransference, 42, 87
  on maternal holding, 199
  on primary maternal
      preoccupation, 65
  on psychosis as disease, 6
  on true and false self, 133
Winnicottian school, 5–7

Zarathustra, 196, 197